Merry Christmas 1750

With much love.

Betty & Jim

THE HIGHER HAPPINESS

BOOKS BY RALPH W. SOCKMAN

The Higher Happiness
Now to Live!
The Fine Art of Using
The Lord's Prayer
Date with Destiny
The Highway of God
Live for Tomorrow
Recoveries in Religion
The Paradoxes of Jesus
The Unemployed Carpenter
Morals of Tomorrow
Men of the Mysteries
Suburbs of Christianity
The Revival of the Conventual Life
  in the Church of England in the Nineteenth Century (thesis)

RALPH W. SOCKMAN

THE HIGHER
HAPPINESS

New York   *Nashville*
ABINGDON-COKESBURY PRESS

THE HIGHER HAPPINESS

SET UP, PRINTED, AND BOUND BY THE PARTHENON PRESS, AT NASHVILLE, TENNESSEE, UNITED STATES OF AMERICA

To KATHY,
*who makes the Beatitudes
more believable*

Foreword

IN HIS "Christmas Oratorio" W. H. Auden satirizes the self-centered trend of so many current religious attitudes in the following prayer:

O God, put away justice and truth for we cannot understand them and we do not want them. Eternity would bore us dreadfully. Leave thy heavens and come down to our earth of waterclocks and hedges. Become our uncle. Look after Baby, amuse Grandfather, . . . help Willie with his homework, introduce Muriel to a handsome naval officer. Be interesting and weak like us, and we will love you as we love ourselves.

The cult of the happiness seekers would reduce God to a Santa Claus who comes down *our* chimneys, to fill *our* stockings with *our* desires. In the midst of the popular man-centered effort to make God our ally rather than our sovereign, this book explores the charter of the higher happiness, as given in the Beatitudes.

I wish to express my deep appreciation to my secretaries, Mrs. Helen V. Putnam and Miss Marion M. Marcy, and to Mrs. W. C. Stevens, for their counsel and co-operation in preparing the manuscript.

RALPH W. SOCKMAN

Contents

Introduction: The Secret of the Higher Happiness   11
    WHOSE WORLD IS REAL?
    NEW SOURCES OF SATISFACTION
    A NEW SENSE OF SECURITY

I. Too Proud to Receive 24
   ' *"Blessed are the poor in spirit: for theirs is the kingdom of heaven."*
    WHEN PRIDE SHUTTERS THE MIND
    WHEN PRIDE LOCKS THE HEART
    WHEN PRIDE WEAKENS THE HAND
    WHEN PRIDE CORRUPTS THE CONSCIENCE

II. Keys to Comfort 40
   "Blessed are they that mourn: for they shall be comforted."
    THE DULLNESS OF THE TEARLESS EYE
    DISCOVERIES IN THE DARK
    THE COMFORT OF THE CLEAN CONSCIENCE
    HEALED BY HEALING
    STRENGTH THROUGH SORROW
    NO SADNESS OF FAREWELL

III. The Most Misunderstood Virtue 61
   "Blessed are the meek: for they shall inherit the earth."
    THE BEGINNING OF MEEKNESS
    WHO ARE THE MEEK?
    STRENGTH AT ITS STRONGEST
    WHAT DO THE MEEK GET?

IV. Making Good Wishes Work 76
   "Blessed are they which do hunger and thirst after right-eousness: for they shall be filled."
    HUNGER THAT MEANS HEALTH

Righteousness That Means Goodness
The Formula for Fulfillment
Satisfying the Higher Hungers

V. The Mystery of Mercy 98
"*Blessed are the merciful: for they shall obtain mercy.*"
What Is Mercy?
Why Is It So Hard to Be Merciful?
Who Can Be Merciful?
What Happens to the Merciful?

VI. The Heart Has Eyes 117
"*Blessed are the pure in heart: for they shall see God.*"
Having Eyes, See Ye Not?
The Eyes of the Mind
The Eyes of the Heart
The Pure in Heart—Who?
They See God—How?

VII. What the World Seems to Want Most 132
"*Blessed are the peacemakers: for they shall be called the
children of God.*"
Where Peacemaking Begins
Roads to Reconciliation
The Fight for Fellowship
Beyond Peace of Mind

VIII. Having the Right Enemies 153
"*Blessed are they which are persecuted for righteousness'
sake: for theirs is the kingdom of heaven.*"
Why the Persecution?
Revealing the Real Stuff
Souls Not for Sale
Where Goodness Becomes Creative
The Goodly Company of the Gallant

References 171

Introduction: The Secret of The Higher Happiness

IN AMERICA'S Declaration of Independence our founding fathers asserted that we hold certain rights to be inalienable, among them being "life, liberty, and the pursuit of happiness." Those three rights would seem to be almost inseparable. Having been brought into the world without our consent, we claim the right to live; and life to be worth living must be free to seek its own fulfillment. We crave happiness; we demand it as our right; we pursue it with all our power. And yet the very frequency of our discussions reveals that most of us feel ourselves missing all too much of it.

When happiness seems so elusive, are we mortals justified in claiming it as our due? The basic aim of Gautama Buddha was to suppress not only selfishness but all human desire. His search was for an escape from life rather than for the enjoyment of it. The Greek Stoics tended toward the conclusion that life truly worth living is possible only to the few rare souls. Expectations of happiness by-passed the plain people.

Jesus, however, looked upon all men as children of the heavenly Father, and therefore entitled to share in the joys of life. In his first synagogue appearance he announced that he was divinely commissioned "to preach the gospel to the poor, . . . to heal the brokenhearted, to preach deliverance to the captives, and recovering of sight to the blind, to set at liberty them that are bruised, to preach the acceptable

11

year of the Lord." Quite naturally, Jesus' hearers at first welcomed him as a herald of happiness. His collected sayings, as reported by Matthew and called the Sermon on the Mount, begin with a list of eight ways to be happy.

The Beatitudes, however, run so counter to the current ideas of happiness that men find them hard to believe. Some would explain them as applying only to that perfect kingdom which is to be consummated in the age beyond history. But as Toynbee reminds us, "the divine 'Other World' transcends the earthly life of man without ceasing to include it." Since "the Kingdom of God is within you" as well as a future social consummation, its rules of happiness have a relevance here and now.

Nor can we dissolve our difficulty in believing the Beatitudes by divorcing the word "blessed" from the word "happy." Admittedly the latter term as commonly used is too light a vehicle to carry the full meaning of the biblical word "blessed." But Carlyle was oversimplifying when he wrote: "There is in man something more than the love of happiness. We can do without happiness and instead find blessedness." To talk about being blessed without being happy is to announce a hymn without starting the tune. Jesus saw and shared men's longing for happiness. He did not give them a stone when they asked for bread. He met men on the plane of their desires and lifted them to the level of their needs. He filled their dreams with richer and higher happiness.

Whose World Is Real?

The first requisite for being happy is to settle the seat of sovereignty in one's life. Every social organism, if it is to function effectively, must determine the place of final authority. Jesus made much of this point. He declared: "No servant can serve two masters"; and "if a house be divided against itself, that house cannot stand."

Not only must every life be integrated around some central sovereign authority, but, according to Jesus, that sovereign must be God. "Seek ye first the Kingdom of God." To Jesus, God was the center of reference in all things and at all times. He viewed every situation as to how it would affect his heavenly Father. He looked up to God. He so completely yielded his will to God that his wishes were at one with God's. Jesus was therefore in the Kingdom of God and the Kingdom of God was in him even while he was climbing the hills of Galilee.

And we, too, can be in the Kingdom of God while we walk the streets of Cleveland or Chicago. All we need to do is to make God sovereign in our lives, to test everything we do by reference to him, to put his interest before all else. Then the Kingdom of Heaven is within us.

But with most of us, the sovereign is not God but self. The individual's thought runs thus: "I look out for Number One, and that is myself. When a situation arises, my first thought is how it will affect me. Oh to be sure, I should like to have a better world, but my primary concern is to secure a better place in the world that is. I want to see people happy, but first of all I want to be happy myself. I pray for world peace, but my deeper prayer is that I may be secure and undisturbed."

Hence when Christ confronts us with his gospel of happiness, it is his Kingdom of God against our kingdoms of self. The principles of his Kingdom are viewed from the perspective of the kingdom of Smith, the kingdom of Jones, the kingdom of Sockman. And when Jesus says, "Happy are the

meek, for they shall inherit the earth," or "Happy are they
that mourn, for they shall be comforted," we in our little
worlds of the self exclaim: "What an impractical dreamer
Jesus was. His way may be lovely in some future Utopia, but
it will not work in our world of reality."

But which is the real world, the one Jesus saw or the one
we see? A few years ago a room in New York's Museum
of Natural History was arranged in accordance with the
way it was supposed to look to a dog entering the door.
Just how an interior decorator knows the way things look
to a dog, I am not quite sure! In this particular room, however,
the legs of the table were made to resemble large pillars, the
chairs were lofty thrones, and the mantel above the fireplace
appeared as an unscalable precipice high overhead.

Which was reality, the room as it looked to a dog, or the
room as it looked to a man? Being men, we say of course
that the room as we see it is the real one. But may there not
be a divine eye as much above ours in perception as ours
is above the dog's? And may not our little worlds as we see
them seem as grotesque to the God above as the dog's room
looks to us?

And is it not logical to say that the most truly "real" world
is the world as it looks to God who created it? That is the
world Jesus saw more clearly than any other being who ever
trod this earth, because he was at one with his Heavenly
Father. He laid down the rules for living in the real world
as he saw it, that is, in the Kingdom of God; and we reveal
ourselves as spiritual and mental yokels when we ridicule
those principles as impractical just because they do not seem
to fit our little man-viewed world. It was said of the apostolic
Christians that they were the men who turned the world up-

side down. In reality Jesus' teachings turned the world right side up.

Jesus knew that the ideas of happiness contained in the Beatitudes would seem foolish to the world. They belong to that company of truths which are hidden from "the wise and prudent." He uttered them not to the crowd but to his little group of disciples, because he knew they would be intelligible only to those who had been initiated into the mysteries of the Kingdom. He whispered his Beatitudes into the ears of the faithful, and they have been overheard by the world, which is haunted by their promise though it hesitates to accept their program.

If we are to enter into the secret of the higher happiness pictured by Jesus, the first step is to change the seat of sovereignty from self to God. The old evangelists were wont to exhort their hearers to "get right with God." To many that meant merely confessing their sins, pleading forgiveness, and then starting with a clean slate. It does mean that, and then more. To get right with God means to make him the sovereign of our lives and to seek first his Kingdom. It means that in any situation our first thought is of God rather than of self. To get right with God means that we look up to him as a Father whose will we desire to do, and not as a Santa Claus whose gifts will serve our purposes. It means that we use prayer as a boatman uses a boat hook, to pull the boat to the shore and not to try to pull the shore to the boat.

If the conditions of happiness sketched in the Beatitudes seem too far removed from the realities of our world, let us remember Donald Baillie's word in *God Was in Christ*:

To detach the ethic from the whole context of the Christian secret is to make it irrelevant because it is impossible. The main function of the impossible ethic is to drive us away from our-selves to God; and then there grows that peculiar kind of good-ness which can never be achieved by mere moral endeavor, the Christian kind, which is all unconscious of itself and gives all to the glory of God.

New Sources of Satisfaction

When the seat of sovereignty is settled in God, new sources of happiness begin to appear in our lives.

Maurice Maeterlinck, who demonstrated his initiation into the mysteries of happiness by his drama *The Blue Bird*, flashes another revealing light on the subject in his study of Mary Magdalene. In it he makes Mary say of Jesus: "He brings a happiness that was not known before, and all those who come near him are happy, it seems, like children at their waking."

When a normal, happy infant opens its eyes from sleep, the haze of dreams seems to linger in its gaze, leaving the ob-server to wonder what images had been lurking behind the closed blinds of those eyes in slumber. A brightening aware-ness begins to break through the fog of half-awakeness. The clearing eyes turn this way and that in a sort of wonder, as if they were exploring their little world for the first time. And then if they catch the eye of a loving mother looking over the edge of the crib, through the smile of recognition there shines a light never seen on land or sea before.

So, says Mary, Christ brings to men a happiness like that of children at their waking. When we first wake up to Christ's world, where God is sovereign, there is the fog of dream in our eyes. We look at Christ with his promises of happiness to the poor in spirit, the meek, the mourners, and we say, "Can his be the real world, or is it only the fancy of a lovely dream?" But the longer we look at Christ and love him and follow him, the more real his world becomes—and the more wonders and beauties begin to appear.

New meanings and values are seen in old familiar things. Nature is revealed as the very garment of God, not only fascinating in itself, but deeply symbolic of the divine love behind it. And if we could attune our thoughts to God as completely as did Francis of Assisi, we should discover a new and rewarding kinship with the dumb animals. His contemporaries put Francis down as a bit simple when they saw him running around "brothering" the poor beasts; but now that the pompous prelates and emblazoned crusaders of his day have long been forgotten, the spirit of the saint still shines with a light that time does not dim. Whose world was the more real, that of Francis or that of the worldly wise who ridiculed him?

When Jesus was trying to initiate his hearers into the secret of his higher happiness by setting them to "seek first the kingdom of God," he bade them go out and behold the fowls of the air. His prescription still holds. Listen to the bird singing among the leafy branches of the tree. What does it care whether anyone sees or hears it? Does that bird seem to worry about any other songster's surpassing it? Apparently it just sings "to its heart's content." Ah, that's it, it sings to its heart's content. The bird is created to sing, and it finds satisfaction in singing, because it thus fulfills its true nature.

Yonder is a young woman in love, going about her work indifferent to its drudgery, oblivious of any observers. She, too, is singing to her heart's content. In love she has found a channel through which she can pour out her heart, and by a divine paradox thereby she discovers the springs which fulfill her nature. Love is blind, we say. Yes, blind to some disagreeable things that are seen and temporal, but awake to new things which are unseen and eternal.

And when human love is placed under God's sovereignty, it is lifted to higher levels of happiness. In some of the homes of our godly grandfathers there hung framed mottoes like this: "Christ is the head of this house." Such legends have gone out of fashion. But whenever the words in those frames are really written on the hearts in the home, family life takes on a new fullness of shared interests, and a new firmness of mutual loyalties. When friendship is set in the frame of divine love, new bonds of appreciation are begotten and a more understanding reverence for personality is developed. When God is given priority, work takes on new purpose and satisfaction, all life gains new depth and richness.

When we awake to such new sources of happiness, there wells up in us an overflowing sense of gratitude. This quickens the desire to serve; and when we start serving, we are lifted out of our little kingdoms of self into new satisfactions, seemingly inexhaustible. If we seek happiness through what we can take in, we soon reach a surfeit. We get "fed up," as we say. A young American girl was checking out of a hotel in Venice. As she paid her bill, she said to the man at the desk, "I wish I could stay on here forever, enjoying this wonder city." He smiled indulgently, and replied, "You would get tired of it." A tourist soon tires of even the most exotic place. One cannot keep on just taking in sights or thrills or applause or anything else without becoming bored. But that young woman can return from Venice to some plain little American town, put her love into a family, her life into a community, and find a satisfaction which grows with her self-giving.

Writing of Bunyan's Valiant-for-truth, George Bernard

Shaw says: "This is the true joy in life, the being used for a purpose recognized by yourself as a weighty one, . . . the being a force of Nature instead of a feverish little clod of ailments and grievances complaining that the world will not devote itself to making you happy." Shaw's insight, like Bunyan's, catches a primary secret of the higher happiness.

To be used of God rather than to use him, to comfort rather than to seek comfort, to give love rather than to ask for love—such should be the direction of our desiring. This principle, which seems a truism to Christ's followers, needs emphasis in a day when the cult of happiness is displacing the divine gospel of happiness. A popular psychology of success is presented by many pulpits in the name of religion. How to use God for the satisfaction of our own self-interests, how to make him an ally in our campaigns for personal popularity and business prosperity, all this is very pleasing to modern congregations, who call it good, practical, down-to-earth preaching. That is its defect. It is down to earth rather than up to God.

Christ came to save men, not to satisfy them. And the core of his saving gospel is that by self-forgetting we find, by giving we receive. We must make God our sovereign before he can become our servant. When we move our minds and hearts from the kingdom of self to the Kingdom of God, the secrets and sources of the higher happiness begin to reveal themselves.

A New Sense of Security

Moreover, when we make God sovereign, we are immune to so many "ills that flesh is heir to." The higher happiness which he imparts is above the reach of many changes on the surface of things.

We live much at the mercy of events. Some untoward incident in the morning puts a dent in our composure for the entire day. A sharp word of criticism leaves a wound which festers for hours. Our faith in the triumph of righteousness fluctuates with the reports of the news column. It is unreal to say that we can become absolutely independent of environmental changes. The more refined the person, the more sensitive he is to his surroundings. The more we love, the more points there are at which we can be wounded. Jesus was affected by his environment. He wept in sympathy with the sorrow of Mary and Martha and at the distress of his beloved Jerusalem. But it is one thing to be moved by events; it is another to be mastered by them. And in the very shadow of his Cross, our Lord said: "Be of good cheer, I have overcome the world."

A peace and happiness so secure can come only to those who are initiated into the secrets of the Kingdom of God. When a person makes God sovereign and, like the Son of man, seeks to minister rather than to be ministered unto, many of the anxieties about rewards and recognition disappear, many petty insults and criticisms lose their sting, many rivalries and comparisons and envies vanish. The man who walks with God, his mind on high thoughts, becomes a Gulliver unbound by the pygmies of Lilliput, unharried by efforts to "keep up with the Joneses." He who looks to God for his values and listens to the still small voice of conscience rather than to the clamor of the crowd enjoys the security voiced by the psalmist: "Thou shalt hide them in the secret place of thy presence from the pride of man: thou shalt keep them secretly in a pavilion from the strife of tongues."

Henry James in *The Portrait of a Lady* draws the picture of a young dilettante who was not making a go of life.

Unable to get what he wanted, he sought to make others think he had what they wanted. He posed as a refined recluse. A rich young woman mistook this pose as the sign of spirituality and married him. After he got control of her purse, the fellow set up house in a palace in Rome, where he entertained distinguished guests in order that he might have the pleasure of excluding the lesser folk who craved to be invited. The man's whole pleasure consisted in making others envy him. Some people value what they have only in proportion to how much others want it. The higher happiness of Kingdom-living is above all such enslavement to circumstance.

Furthermore, Christlike contentment is largely above the reach of physical ailment. As a healer, Jesus knew the actuality of bodily pain. He did not ignore the body; he mastered it. His followers have found the power whereby they can say: "I keep under my body, and bring it into subjection." Recently a blind man was introduced to me. I could hardly have told that he was sightless by anything he said or by the expression of his face. I have since learned his story. He is a leading executive in a large industry. When he lost his sight in the prime of his life, he determined not to allow his blindness to affect his spirits. He is still a leader in the civic, cultural, and religious life of his city. His whole attitude reveals that he has triumphed over what others would call a tragedy. He is but one of a mighty host who have found through their faith a peace and power which physical ills could not shatter.

Still further, the higher happiness has a security which withstands the ravages of time. Charles Carroll Albertson tells of an interview granted by Cecil Rhodes, in his later years. The interviewer congratulated the empire-builder of South Africa on his success. "You ought to be happy," said the man.

Cecil Rhodes replied, "Happy. Good Lord, no!" Then he went on to say that he had spent all his life amassing a fortune, only to find that he now had to spend it all, half on doctors to keep him out of the grave, and the other half on lawyers to keep him out of jail. The answer, to be sure, was touched with humor and hyperbole, but it points the proverbial truth that worldly achievement does not insure happiness. Many discover their lofty monuments turning to dust even before they die.

Our feeling of contentment is extremely sensitive to the calendar. We number our days, not that we may apply our hearts unto wisdom, but that we may give our minds unto worry. When, however, we get right with God by making him sovereign, we begin to lay up treasures in his Kingdom, "where neither moth nor rust doth corrupt." If our satisfactions depend on the state of our minds and hearts rather than on the state of our bodies or our bank accounts, then time does not tarnish our happiness, for we have something which we can take with us. We do not spoil our enjoyment of the present by fearfully counting how many years are left to us before we have to leave our possessions.

Shortly before his death, the late Edward Madison Cameron in whimsical but delightful fashion delivered a little lecture to his aging body, from which he was about to part:

When you can go no further, I shall leave you and be free. . . . When we separate I shall continue to exist. . . . A power greater than you and I started us on our journey. Your journey is approaching its end and you are aware of it. My journey has merely begun, and I know it because I have never been more alive. Our separation is therefore not one of sadness but of joy. You are weary and want to stop. I am longing to alight from this slowing vehicle and go on without you.

The man who can write thus about death manifests that he has found a peace that comes from adjustment to God rather than to the world. The popular conception of peace of mind is all too much a matter of smooth alignment with things that are "seen and temporal." But the fashion of this world passes away. Lasting personal peace must be sought in adjustment to the "things that are unseen and eternal."

There is a "peace of God which passeth all understanding" of the world, but its secret is comprehended by those who have been initiated into the Kingdom of God and have remained in the fraternity of the faithful. Theirs is the higher happiness.

I. Too Proud to Receive

Blessed are the poor in spirit:
for theirs is the kingdom of heaven.

BENJAMIN FRANKLIN has told us the exercise by which he once tried to attain moral perfection. He drew up a list of the twelve virtues which he thought embodied the essential traits of a good life. He kept a little book in which a page was allotted to each virtue. Then he ruled each page with seven lines, one for each day of the week. His program was to focus his mind on one virtue a week at a time, keeping track of each daily violation. Thus he went through the list, thinking that since his conscience told him what was right and what was wrong, he could attain the good and avoid the bad.

When he showed his list to an old Quaker friend, he was gently informed that he had omitted the virtue of humility. Franklin added it at once. His list then read as follows: temperance, silence, order, resolution, frugality, industry, sincerity, justice, moderation, cleanliness, tranquility, chastity, humility.

Ben Franklin's homely wisdom and practical counsel have made him an oft-quoted guide in our search for successful living. But while his precepts make for adjustment and advancement in our relations with men, they differ in spiritual depth and emphasis from those given by the great Hebrew prophets and Jesus of Nazareth.

Take this matter of humility. Franklin put it last in his list of virtues. But Jesus put it first in his Beatitudes: "Blessed are the poor in spirit: for theirs is the kingdom of heaven." And Christian theology has pretty consistently put pride as the first and most basic of the deadly sins. Augustine, sixteen centuries ago, asked, "What could begin this evil will, but pride, that is the beginning of all sin?" And C. S. Lewis in our day declares: "Pride leads to every other vice; it is the complete anti-God state of mind. . . . Pride is spiritual cancer; it eats up the very possibility of love, or contentment, or even common sense."

Humility, then, is not just an added grace which adorns man's other virtues to make them more presentable and likable. It is the foundation of all other virtues. Pride is not just a flaw on the surface of life, which mars the appearance of men's virtues; it is the basic sin at the bottom of all our wrongdoing.

The reason that pride is the primary sin is suggested in the words: "God resisteth the proud and giveth grace to the humble." That statement is paralleled in word and proven in works on many pages of Scripture. The principle here revealed is this: Pride is the basic sin because it begets a resistance that stops growth toward God; humility is the primary virtue because it possesses a grace of receptivity which makes for growth.

WHEN PRIDE SHUTTERS THE MIND

Pride is basic because it is related to the original roots of man's nature. Human beings, like all living creatures, have a vitality which pushes them out to preserve themselves. The little child takes its first step, and then looks around wth pride for the applause of its elders. Later the boy brings home from school his report card, and both he and his parents take a justifiable pride in his progress. Such pride seems a legitimate part of our native motive power. Where then is the point at which pride develops divine resistance?

We sometimes say about a certain person that his learning has "gone to his head." Of course, that is where learning is supposed to go! But in this case, it seems to have gotten there with wrong results. The person has become intoxicated with his own achievement. When pride "goes to the head," it inflates the ego with such self-importance that the man fails to see the import of things around him. He becomes so proud of his own opinions that he argues to show how right he is rather than discusses to find out what is right. He talks when he should be listening. He is arrogant in his judgments and uncharitable toward those who differ with him. He closes the shutters of his mind against the light of new truth, which might reveal the dust that has settled on his cherished convictions.

As Reinhold Niebuhr points out, all human knowledge has an ideological taint, that is, it tends to form a pattern of ideas and then the pattern tends to stop the growth of truth. That was the situation Jesus faced in the scholars of his day. The scribes and Pharisees had built up a system of doctrine which the newcomer, Jesus of Nazareth, did not fit. They scornfully asked whence came the carpenter's knowledge.

Certainly we in our time have been made familiar with these idea-patterns. We call them ideologies. We talked about the conflict of ideologies in World War II between the Nazi totalitarianism and our free societies. And now we speak of another clash of ideologies between Communism and capitalism. But if we are true to the spirit of Christ, we do not try to pit our patterns of ideas against another set of patterns but rather we try to turn on the light of truth which will show up falsity wherever found. Jesus heralded the coming of the Spirit of Truth of whom he said, "He will guide you into all truth." Christ is our eternal guide, "the same yesterday, and today, and forever," for the very reason that he did not give patterns of truth, but paths to truth. He gave directions rather than definitions. And directions are never outgrown.

The proud man closes his mind with patterns, with preconceptions, with prejudices. Thus God resists him because he is too proud to receive the truth.

But God "giveth grace to the humble." Just as the head of wheat which is filled with the best grain bends on its stalk, so the mind which is best filled bows humbly, realizing that the more it knows, the more there is to know. Charles Kettering, whose name has become a household word because of his contributions to science and industry, attributes his progress to what he calls "intelligent ignorance." The hope of advance lies in those who are intelligent enough to be aware of their ignorance. Thomas Huxley once wrote to Charles Kingsley: "Sit down before the facts as a little child, be prepared to give up every preconceived notion, follow humbly wherever Nature leads, or you shall learn nothing. I have only begun to learn content and peace of mind since I have resolved at all risks to do this."

Would we be humble enough to receive the grace of God in this matter of truth? Then we must modestly admit that the truth as it is in God is too vast for us to claim a monopoly for ourselves or our group. Whether we be Protestant or Roman Catholic, Presbyterian or Methodist, we must humbly hear our Lord as he says, "Other sheep I have which are not of this fold." We must face facts with the open mind of a child, willing to follow where the truth leads, cost what it may.

Pride of spirit is like the light inside our motor cars. When we turn the light on at night, it transforms the windows of the car into mirrors. We can see our reflection, but we cannot see well to drive. We have to turn off the interior light if we wish to get a clear view of the road ahead.

Pride cannot be cured by one dose of humility. Humility is a medicine to be taken daily, drop by drop. Each day we must study to be open to new ideas, to be patient with opposition, to be ready to listen to reproof, even when we are not convinced that it is deserved, and to be willing to confess our error when it is shown us.

It is reported of Francis of Assisi that he had a simple and effective way of keeping himself humble. Whenever anyone praised his virtues, he would ask a fellow monk to sit down with him and tell him his faults. It might facetiously be said that if Francis had been married, he would have had that service rendered him at home! And in all seriousness, the godly home is the superb training ground for the grace of humility, for there love sees the weakness blended with strength, avoids flattery of the false and cares enough to cure.

The poor in spirit are not poor-spirited, devoid of spark and responsiveness, like the cold engine of a motor car on a winter morning. Nor are they dispirited, with head and heart drooping through disillusionment and discouragement, like the leaves of a frozen plant. They do not despise themselves as worthless worms of the dust, for they have learned of their Lord that they are of immortal value, each one unique and irreplaceable. But realizing that their minds are temples of the Holy Spirit and that their systems of thought even at the best are only broken shafts of the divine Light, they humbly remember that, as Pastor John Robinson told the Pilgrims leaving Holland, the Lord has more light and truth yet to break forth from his Holy Word.

WHEN PRIDE LOCKS THE HEART

Hear a parable from family history. Two brothers in their young manhood jointly managed their father's farm. Property was held in common. But gradually they drew apart. The younger brother prided himself that he was smarter than his older brother and could make more money sitting on the fence than the other could make plowing the fields. Consequently he spent considerable time on the fence. The other felt aggrieved at having to divide up after having done so much of the work. Finally they did divide their holdings. Then for some twenty years until death separated them, they did not speak, although living only a few rods apart. Thus they forfeited that fellowship which can be so fruitful between brothers. And whenever anyone tried to effect a reconciliation between them, the attitude of each was, "I'll not be the first to forgive."

How varied and numerous are the situations in which pride locks the heart against the love and life which might be received. Consider the pride involved in age consciousness. Adults may become so proud of their experience and attainments that they condescendingly shut out the contributions which youth might make to their lives. And young people on their side often show, to use Dr. Geoffrey Fisher's phrase, "that courteous contempt which youth has for age." The younger set so frequently assume that in this fast-moving era parents do not understand the interests and problems of their children. The late John Buchan, Governor-General of Canada, recalled the inspiration he received as a young lawyer in London from association with older members of the bar, and deplored the modern tendency to segregate professional and social groups along age lines. When the spirit of the Lord gives the grace of humility, "your old men shall dream dreams and your young men shall see visions" and they shall do it together, each age enriching the other.

And what prisoners family pride can make! Yonder lives a woman who boasts of herself as belonging to one of the "first families" of the town. Her conversation is burdened with complaints about the deterioration of the town's population. She idealizes the past, ever telling of "the good old days." Her little bird-like soul sits ensconced in the branches of her family tree, twittering around the nest she did not build, keeping aloof from the people she might learn to know and like, leaving undone the service she might render to her community, and missing the contribution her town might make to her.

Or think how the pride of race poisons human relationships. When a person has nothing else of which to be proud, he can always fall back on his race, provided, of course that he is white and Aryan. And how much of our race prejudice is fomented by people who have little else but race to distinguish them!

Or consider the form of pride which we call vanity. Vanity is shallow pride, manifest in small ways and on slight grounds. The vain person preens himself before every show window that he passes. By turning windows into mirrors he keeps seeing himself when he ought to be seeing the things around him. Thus pride makes him a prisoner of himself. The person who gets stuck *on* himself is stuck *with* himself. He has himself on his hands, for nobody else wants him.

Or take the pride of achievement which separates a person from God. The record of King Uzziah illustrates it. Listen: "His name spread far abroad; for he was marvelously helped, till he was strong. But when he was strong, his heart was lifted up to his own destruction." Similar statements occur again and again in Old Testament biography. Success breeds a sense of self-sufficiency. Men no longer feel the need of God. Then they fall.

When men are thus lifted up in heart, God resists their pride. And that resistance shows itself in the contraction of their own natures and the reduction of their natural enjoyments. Self-centered persons see only what affects their own interests. The only music they enjoy is the blowing of their own horns. Extreme but not too unusual is the writer who had been regaling a little group with a running account of his own activities and achievements. Finally he stopped and said: "Enough about myself. Let's hear from you. What do you think of my latest book?" When a person so lives in the kingdom of self, he is shut out of the kingdom of heaven.

In contrast with this pride of the heart, the poor in spirit have the grace of humility. They are not egocentric, viewing everything in the light of how it affects them. They are not egotistical, projecting themselves into every situation, concerned always about their position and prestige. Not feeling that they merit the spotlight as star performers, they are content with a minor role or even a job behind the scenes, provided the play goes on.

Having emptied themselves of space-wasting egoism, they have room for the interests of those around them. By becoming interested in others, they become interesting to others. Thus they open the traffic of mind and heart and are delivered from the isolation of self-centeredness. And this satisfaction which comes to those who forget themselves is part of the kingdom of heaven.

Another factor which helps to make the poor in spirit divinely happy is that they are not sensitive about getting their so-called rights. Not being proud and self-important, they are not forever feeling hurt when recognition is not accorded them. Not inflated by egoism, they are not frequently bruised. And they do not cherish grudges. If men keep believing the world to be their enemy, it becomes so. If they keep thinking others are cheating them, the very belief cheats them out of their peace of mind and many possible friendships. But the poor in spirit are freed from this fretfulness born of sensitive pride. Concerned about the right rather than about their rights, they are immune to petty insults and little anxieties over recognition and rank. And such immunity to uneasiness is a part of the kingdom of heaven.

Moreover, the poor in spirit are helped toward happiness by a deep spirit of gratitude. Modestly feeling that they do not deserve much from God, they see his goodness in even the smallest blessings. This does not mean, however, that they reduce their relations with God to small scale, dwelling on little details. They expect great things from God, but they do not claim them as their own deserts. The poor in spirit recall how long they have been on the receiving end of life. Their minds run back to their childhood when parents sat beside their crumby beds and held their feverish hands. As they rummage among their memories, they uncover the many forgotten reasons for gratitude.

Professor Henry N. Wieman suggests that each of us should keep a mental rosary of his most precious memories, including the beauty he has seen, the fellowship he has enjoyed, and the good gifts which life has brought him. His suggestion is that we should frequently count the beads on this mental rosary and give thanks to God for each separate favor. When we start such a chain of memory, we find it reaching all the way back to Calvary and beyond. And our hearts well up with unspeakable gratitude.

The human race can roughly be divided into two groups: those who think they are giving more than they get, and those who think they are getting more than they give. The former are ever talking about their sacrifices, and every gift which they make seems a burden. The latter, who are the poor in spirit, feel their indebtedness to the common life around them, "both to the Greeks, and to the Barbarians; both to the wise, and to the unwise." They set their lives and possessions in the warming sunlight of God's goodness until the icicled springs of their hearts are melted, and the frozen channels of their unforgiving spirits are opened, and spring comes to the wintry soul. Then with George Matheson they turn in humble gratitude to God's limitless love, saying:

> I give thee back the life I owe
> That in thine ocean depths its flow
> May richer, fuller be.

When Pride Weakens the Hand

Bertrand Russell declares: "Of the infinite desires of man, the chief are the desires for power and glory. They are not identical though closely allied."

The desire for power is a part of life's motive power. Our minds and bodies seek increased power over their environment. Thus we grow. Education aims to extend our human energies and controls. The engineer studies to master the physical forces of nature, to harness its streams, even its atoms. The lawyer learns the intricacies of litigation that he may see the elements of a case in true proportion and have the power of cogent appeal in the courtroom. The surgeon cultivates the skill which can cut within a hair's breadth of a vital organ, and earns the patient's gratitude and his own self-respect by his curative power.

It is legitimate to take pride *in* our work. The danger starts when we begin to take pride to ourselves *from* our work. Jesus gave the corrective principle when he said: "Let your light so shine before men, that they may see your good works, and *glorify your Father which is in heaven.*" Albrecht Dürer wrote to a critic who had found fault with some of his work, "It cannot be done better." Yet Dürer was not an egoist. He felt himself an instrument of God, and his concern was with the truth he was interpreting rather than with his own reputation. What is our main motive, to make something *of* ourselves or to make something *through* ourselves?

A conversation is reported between Herbert Spencer and Thomas Huxley. The former said: "I suppose that all one can do with one's life is to make one's mark and die." Huxley replied: "It is not necessary to make one's mark; all one need do is to give a push." The poor in spirit are not worried about the mark they are making. They are content to give a push, even though they be hidden behind the cause they are advancing. They have push, but they are not "pushers," elbowing their way to the front. Whatever success they may achieve, they attribute to sources beyond themselves.

To survive defeat is a real achievement. It calls for courage, pluck, perseverance, faith. But to survive victories is even harder. We have a common saying that "nothing succeeds like success." That seems true in the short view. Business begets business, crowds draw crowds, prosperity has a cumulative attraction. But when we take the longer perspective of history, we see that nothing fails like success. Worldly men and worldly things cannot stand success. Only godly men and godly things can survive victories.

After World War II, the victorious nations became concerned about the re-education of Germany and Japan. Deputations of educators were put at the task. A defeated nation usually recognizes that its methods must have been wrong. It is open-minded to the study of new techniques. But a victorious country feels sure its leaders and tactics must have been right. Hence it often continues them to the point of a static conservatism, which paves the way for future defeat. Wellington's prestige and influence tended toward the repetition of outmoded traditions. And the French army, victorious in World War I, clung to its patterns until its Maginot Line was rendered useless by Hitler's new and more mobile type of warfare.

The poor in spirit not only possess a resiliency of spirit which keeps them from being crushed by defeat but they have a humility which keeps them open to self-criticism after their victories, and thus prevents just pride from deteriorating into self-exaltation and static self-confidence. The better they become, the farther they feel themselves from their goal.

Moreover, they see that the fruits of victory as well as the roots of victory must be viewed in the light of our dependence on God. Their sense of stewardship keeps them from misusing the power achieved through success. Individuals, groups, nations get power. Then they abuse it. Then they lose it. In Czarist Russia the privileged classes, even the church, ceased to serve. They trod on the poor until the peasants rose up and replaced them. And Communism bids fair to undo itself by the same principle. It makes its appeal to people who want something material which they do not have. But suppose that Communism should succeed in producing such a multiplicity

of things that it changed the economy of scarcity into an economy of plenty. Poor people can be regimented upward by the
principle of self-interest. But affluent persons cannot be regimented downward by the same principle. As long as Communism is based on material self-interest, it cannot stand success. It will eventually lose the hearts of men to "the Son of
Man who came not to be ministered unto but to minister."

The poor in spirit, feeling themselves to be stewards rather
than ultimate owners of victory's fruit, are thus largely freed
from the selfish fear of loss. They are concerned, of course,
about the good and full use of the property for which they
are responsible. But such concern is very different from our
usual financial worries. What do we worry about in our business and money matters? Is it that we are not making the best
use of what we have? Or is it the fear of losing what we have?
Ah, let's be frank. It is wealth for power and pleasure and
prestige that we are so eager to get and so afraid of losing.
How many of our personal worries and how many of the
world's tensions would vanish if we were concerned about
wealth for use rather than wealth for power. Those who are
freed from the inordinate pride of possession are able to travel
light and lightheartedly through the uncertainties of the
market place. And such freedom from anxiety is part of the
Kingdom of Heaven.

Furthermore, this freedom from possessiveness enables the
poor in spirit really to enjoy the persons and objects around
them. We cannot help wanting things; that is our nature.
But what makes the difference is how we want them. Things
are not just means for our use. They are God's handiwork,
worthwhile in themselves, and they are to be treated as such.
And as to persons, we spoil our relationship with a friend
when we try to use him for our own benefit. We continue

to be true friends so long as each desires the good of the other.

Bonaro Overstreet writes of meeting a returned soldier who had been an engineer in the South Pacific during the war. He told her that he had spent much time in that region photographing native birds. He said that his experience had almost made him determined to give up his favorite sport of hunting. It was not that he felt there was anything wrong in hunting,

"but," said he, "when you hunt birds with a gun it's just your own purpose that counts. But when you shoot birds with a camera, you're trying to understand their life . . . trying to catch them doing the things natural to them." Then he added: "I thought a lot about this while I was in the hospital getting my knee fixed up . . . and I kind of got the notion that what's wrong with the world is that we're always looking at people with our own purposes in mind and not caring a hoot what they want or what they're like when they're being themselves."

That young soldier diagnosed one of our major diseases— the spirit of possessiveness which uses others for our own purposes. It is this possessive spirit which so frequently take the luster off marital love. It perverts the relationship between man and God. Too much modern popular religion tries to use God simply as a means of getting what we want—health, happiness, prosperity, and the like. We must remember that God is a Father, and he can shower his love on us when we become true sons to him, not thinking ever of our deserts, not asserting our rights, not trying to use him for our self-centered purposes. Such self-forgetting sons are the poor in spirit.

When Pride Corrupts the Conscience

Pride is so basic a sin because it poisons even our virtues. When a person becomes proud of his purity, he becomes a prude. When he prides himself on his correct behavior, he becomes a prig. When he becomes proud of his righteousness, he is like the Pharisee who thanked God that he was not as other men are, unjust, extortioners, adulterers. And we all remember how Jesus praised by contrast the publican who prayed, "God be merciful to me, a sinner."

But even the publican's humility can be carried to the point of being spoiled by pride. Recently in a New Jersey town a questionnaire was put out among the children in an elementary school. The teachers were apparently trying to discover which pupils needed special attention to develop their social attitudes. One question was, "Which student in the class brags the least about herself?" One little twelve-year-old girl put down her own name. It must have been something like that which St. Jerome had in mind when he said, "Beware of the pride of humility."

There are some persons who make no religious profession. They join no church. And they take a kind of pride in this fact, for they say, "At least we do not pretend to be what we are not." They are, no doubt, sincere, and the virtue of sincerity is one of the noblest. But do not take pride in sincerity when secured by simply taking low aim. Christian humility is attained by aiming at the highest we know with the utmost we have, and then feeling how far short we come of the ideal.

The feeling of strength is very deceitful in the moral realm. How often it happens that a person is weakest at the point where he thinks himself strongest. Good traits of character are in personality somewhat as the grain is in wood. It is the grain which gives beauty to wood, but if you wish to split the wood, just hit it along the grain. Similarly it is along the grain of his good traits that a man's character is most easily cracked.

The poor in spirit are not complacent about their good

points, leaving them unguarded, exposed either to temptation
or to self-righteousness. They keep their consciences sensitive
by constant comparison with the Christ. They bring their
virtues into the Galilean light and view them as cheap stage
jewelry brought out to the sun. They are saved from smugness
by the purity of the Master's sinlessness. In his quickening
presence they see the need of something more dynamic than
mere decency and something more redemptive than respectability. They measure their little kindnesses alongside the sacrifice of the Cross, and cry with Isaac Watts:

> Were the whole realm of nature mine,
>   That were a present far too small;
> Love so amazing, so divine,
>   Demands my soul, my life, my all.

In such contrite and humble hearts the Eternal can dwell.
Thus theirs is the Kingdom of Heaven.

II. Keys to Comfort

Blessed are they that mourn:
for they shall be comforted.

COMMON SENSE is right in holding that not all sorrow is a blessing, even in disguise. Bitter bemoaning which ends in the blind alley of mere remorse is not blessed. If like Napoleon a man follows his star of personal ambition and then sees it set in defeat, his gloomy sorrow brings no more consolation than did the dictator's at St. Helena. Not all tears are profitable. Paul recognizes that there are grades of sorrow when he declares, "For godly sorrow worketh repentance to salvation . . . ; but the sorrow of the world worketh death."

Hence when we seek the sources of comfort we must first consider the causes of our sorrow. What are we mourning for? Is ours a grief or a grievance? Are we childishly crying over spilt milk or pettishly tearful over hurt pride? Is our sorrow rooted in self-centeredness or does it stem from the sufferings of others? Are we painfully penitent for our sins or merely bemoaning their penalties?

Some sorrow may be only effervescing self-pity. The person who goes around pitying himself bores others with the repeated story of his troubles until he is left more and more to himself. So he himself becomes the only audience to whom he can pour out his woes. Thus his troubles poured back into himself foam up like the charged liquids which the druggist pours from one glass to another. Frequently, too, this foaming self-pity is poisoned with bitter resentment. Before seeking

40

the divine prescription for comfort, we should analyze our tears and diagnose our sorrows.

Significantly the second Beatitude with its promise of comfort follows the first Beatitude, with its blessing on the poor in spirit. The quality of our mourning is to be tested by the humility of our minds. Sorrow due to injured pride, to threatened prestige, to thwarted possessiveness, does not receive the promise of divine comfort. But the poor in spirit who mourn for their sins, who feel the sufferings of others, who weep over love's losses—they shall be comforted. Godly sorrow will receive God's consolation.

THE DULLNESS OF THE TEARLESS EYE

However hard it is to believe, "Blessed are they that mourn for they shall be comforted," we cannot jump to the opposite and say, "Blessed are they who never mourn." The eye that never knows tears would lack essential tenderness. The mind that never mourns would not possess the mellowness needed for friendship and love. The heart that never felt a break would not be quite whole.

The Arabs have a saying, "All sunshine makes a desert." If we were always bland, always placidly confident, always smilingly untroubled; if there were no shadows of untoward circumstances, no dark nights of the soul when we toss sleeplessly on our beds trying to see light until the pupils of our mental eyes widen with wonder; if our world contained no difficulties to conquer, no pain to prick our ease, no suffering to call forth our compassion, no unexplained sorrows to accept in faith and love—yes, if our days were all sunshine, our lives would become a desert, our streams of sympathy would dry up, our eyes would become spiritually blind, and our natures swinishly selfish.

When the biologist ranks living creatures in the scale of life, he grades them according to their capacity for pain. At the lowest level are such creatures as the oyster and the worm. The oyster, as we take it from the shell, is alive, but its range of feeling is rated so low that even the most tenderhearted seem never to feel it cruel to bite into an oyster. The turtle is somewhat higher in the scale of life, but the sensitivity of that sluggish animal does not evoke much sympathy. When, however, we rise to the level of the horse, we find a very considerable capacity for pain. The finely bred, high-spirited horse is sensitive not only to the pain of its own body but even to the very mood of its rider. The horse is a mourner among beasts.

When we ascend the animal scale to human beings, we see how the range of suffering has increased. Man has feelings to get hurt, a conscience to gnaw at him, memories to torture him, anxieties to fret him.

> We look before and after,
> And pine for what is not.

And the more highly developed the person, the more sensitive he is to pain and sorrow. A child has its little sorrows, but they are like ripples on a pond, quickly raised and soon subsided. But every increase in capacity to enjoy higher values carries with it growing capacity to suffer. The ear that is most alive to harmony is most hurt by discord. The conscience which is most responsive to goodness is most shocked by the evils around it.

Walt Whitman once became so irritated by the sound of people complaining and whining that he contrasted them with the cows in the field, who do not weep over their sins and losses. But we would not be willing to retreat into bovine complacency in order to escape the pangs of conscience and the pains of sorrow. We would not give up our enjoyment of lovely sunsets and Sistine Madonnas in order that we might be free from the distressing sight of dirty slush and ugly slums.

According to an ancient Greek legend, a woman came down to the River Styx to be ferried across to the region of departed spirits. Charon, the kindly ferryman, reminded her that it was her privilege to drink of the waters of Lethe, and thus forget the life she was leaving. Eagerly she said, "I will forget how I have suffered." "And," added Charon, "remember too that you will forget how you have rejoiced." The woman said, "I will forget my failures." The old ferryman added, "And also your victories." She continued, "I will forget how I have been hated." "And also how you have been loved," added Charon. Then she paused to consider the whole matter, and the end of the story is that she left the draught of Lethe untasted, preferring to retain the memory even of sorrow and failure rather than to give up the memory of life's loves and joys.

The French have a proverb: "To suffer passes away: but to have suffered never passes." The immediate pains and sorrows do pass; but sorrow and suffering bravely borne beget a clarity of vision and a depth of understanding which are an abiding source of comfort.

DISCOVERIES IN THE DARK

"You don't know what things are real in art," said Romain Rolland, "until you come to them in pain; sorrow is the touchstone." That is particularly true in the art of living.

Sorrow is not only the test of reality, but also the spur to its discovery. Many will not bother to learn the truth until driven to it by some dark experience. Mystery and grandeur lie all about us, but most of us do not discover them until trouble or suffering drives us to explore the imprisoning shell in which we have encased ourselves, and then through the crevices we glimpse the heights and depths of life, its beauties as well as its bitterness.

It is against dark velvet that diamonds are displayed to show their luster. It is in the darkness that we discover the richer values of life. Mark you, there is something more involved here than the oft-repeated truism that the night brings out the stars. That sounds passive. But the active principle is that when we face manfully our sorrows and dig into the difficulties, we uncover the "hidden riches of secret places."

The sweetest strains of song and literature are those which tell of saddest thought. Dante and Milton achieved their most luminous insights in periods of deep personal suffering. It was in the winter of their discontent that Tennyson wrote his *In Memoriam* and Browning *The Ring and the Book*, considered by many the noblest works of both men.

Turn from the realm of self-exploration to our social contacts. We do not discover the hidden riches of love and friendship in sunny times. When all is smooth and prosperous, we have fellowship on the more superficial planes of living, in our sports and recreations, in our service clubs and professional societies. We enjoy the camaraderie, we congratulate one another on our successes.

But when sorrow or trouble comes, our relationships run more deeply. When disaster overtakes, men do not always find consolation from their club-mates and fellow golfers. When a heart is breaking in his own home, a doctor does not always go for counsel to his medical colleagues, with whom he is accustomed to discuss his professional cases. More likely he seeks out someone so spiritually close that he can sit down with him in a silence too deep for words. Our most precious relationships are those in which "deep calleth unto deep."

Family ties are strengthened more by the mutual sharing of sorrow than by the enjoyment of prosperity. A husband and wife, who may have been drifting apart on the broad stream of worldly success, are often drawn together when the channel of their lives runs through "the valley of the shadow of death" beside the grave of a beloved child. Not by making homes more comfortable do we lower the divorce rate. Alas, quite the opposite. We could, however, reduce the number of broken homes by making them more comforting.

When we lift our gaze from the realm of our intimate fellowship to the larger sphere of citizenship, we see further evidence of the principle that the "hidden riches of secret places" are discovered in the dark times of suffering. In early New England, our American forefathers on Thanksgiving Day had a custom of putting five grains of corn at each place around the table. This was to remind the observers that during the first dismal winter at Plymouth the food of the Pilgrims was so depleted that only five grains of corn were rationed to each individual at a time. And at one period of that first fateful year, there were only seven healthy colonists able to nurse the sick, and half their original number lay dead. The first settlers of this nation knew what it cost to be an American, and hence they appreciated the values of this land.

In the present America of comparative plenty and security, so many of the inhabitants are the spoiled children of a bountiful civilization. They lack appreciation of the privileges for which they have not had to suffer.

Religion in America is a parasite without roots. The questions that have occupied Europe from the dawn of her history, for which she has fought more fiercely than for empire or liberty, for which she has fasted in deserts, agonized in cells, suffered on the cross, and at the stake, for which she has sacrificed wealth, health, ease, intelligence, life, these questions of the meaning of the world, the origin and destiny of the soul, the life after death, the existence of God, and his relation to the universe, for the American people simply do not exist. They are as inaccessible, as impossible to them, as the Sphere to the dwellers in Flatland. Their healthy and robust intelligence confines itself to the things of this world. Their religion, if they have one, is what I believe they call healthy-mindedness.

The above description drawn by an Englishman seems unfair and irritating to us of America. And most probably the author would revise his picture in the light of the service rendered by the United States to the nations of Western Europe in the last forty years. But it can hardly be denied that our conventional religious faith lacks the depth due to sacrifice and suffering.

A recent survey conducted by a popular American magazine reveals that 95 per cent of those interviewed assert belief in God while only 39 per cent declared that their religious beliefs had any real effect on their political and business attitudes. In summing up the situation, the reviewers said: "The success of Communism is a result of the failure of Christians who have forgotten the revolutionary demands of their faith. And this survey suggests specifically that the weakness of America's position stems from the self-satisfaction of its people, who assume that they are quite as virtuous as anyone can be, and love their fellowman as much as anyone should."

Such superficial religion does not offer the "hidden riches" of comfort. It praises the Bible as God's word, but it has not handled the Book after the manner of those saintly souls whose well-worn Scriptures attest that they have found God "a very present help in time of trouble."

We talk about the grace of God. But do we know it? When Paul kept praying to have his physical ailment, his thorn in the flesh, removed, it still remained; but Paul found the grace of God sufficient to bear it. We have to live and love and suffer our way into the discovery of God's grace. Speaking personally, may I say that during the last decade of my life, things have happened to me which I cannot explain, nor can I say they were all sent of God. When I read, "All things work together for good to them that love God," the only way I can understand this in my own case is after the analogy of a ship. There are parts of a ship which taken by themselves would sink. The engine would sink. The propeller would sink. But when the parts of a ship are built together they float. So with the events of my life. Some have been tragic. Some have been happy. But when they are all built together, they form a craft that floats. Aye, more, one that I believe is going someplace. And I am comforted.

THE COMFORT OF THE CLEAN CONSCIENCE

When Jesus said, "Blessed are they that mourn," he must have had in mind sorrow for one's sin. Perhaps that was his major emphasis, since this Beatitude follows his blessing on "the poor in spirit." Yet when we read these words about mourning, of what do we first think? Sorrow for our sins or sorrow for our losses and sufferings? Very likely it is the latter. And this fact reflects the current religious trend toward being more concerned with the evils that befall us than with the sins we commit.

In certain earnest congregations of an earlier day there was talk of the "mourners' bench," where penitent persons waited for divine pardon. The modern church is more likely to have a psychology clinic where parishioners come to "unpack their hearts with words." To be sure, our gracious God desires no gloomy devotees. Jesus is recorded as saying: "These things have I spoken unto you, that my joy might remain in you, and that your joy might be full." But this promise follows his assertion, "Now ye are clean through the word which I have spoken unto you." Deep and abiding comfort and joy come only to those of a clean and contrite heart.

The crowd craves the promises of God's blessings but without the pain of divine purging. We desire sermons that tell us how to win friends and succeed in business, how to be magnetic personalities and likable companions, how to have peace of mind and forget our fears. Such prescriptions have their temporary value, but let them not be mistaken for the saving gospel. We do not cure sin merely by cushioning ourselves against its consequences. Christ came to make men good rather than merely to make them feel good. Mr. Dooley said: "It is my business to comfort the afflicted and afflict the comfortable." A pretty good role!

To mourn for our sins should not lead to a morbid pessimism, but it does keep us from a shallow optimism. "The Lord is longsuffering, and of great mercy, forgiving iniquity and transgression, and by no means clearing the guilty." God is not to be thought of as a coddling and indulgent grandfather. He is a God of justice, who oversees everything and overlooks nothing, but also a God of grace, who follows us not as police inspector Javert followed Jean Valjean but as a good parent follows through with a wayward child. Ours is a God who rules by the law of love and not by the whim of arbitrary desire, not capriciously cruel one day and softly indulgent the next. He is firm, not condoning our faults, but also faithful, not forgetting our virtues. He is of infinite compassion, under-standing the innermost ache of sorrow and the subtlest causes of failure.

Until we become truly and earnestly sorry for our sins, until we mourn for our misdoings even more than for the evils done to us, we cannot enter into the secret of divine comfort. "Blessed are they that mourn" for their sins with a truly re-pentant spirit, for they shall become better rather than bitter.

Healed by Healing

There is no virtue in pain for the sake of pain. The Great Physician gave much of his energy to the relief of physical ills, and his teaching would seem to urge that his followers use all available resources to prevent accidents, banish disease, and heal suffering. And if we caught his healthy-mindedness, we should regard many of our sorrows and troubles as unreal.

But despite our best precautions, there still remain some pain and suffering. Life comes with pain, the pangs of birth. Life enlarges with pain, our growing pains. Love, the most beautiful thing in life, carries in its nature the possibilities of the most exquisite torture, sometimes burning with desire, sometimes aching with anxiety, sometimes freezing with des-pair. Into the most sheltered circles of circumstance and into the most comfortable philosophy of life, pain probes its way.

The question, then, is how we are to meet this inescapable pain and suffering. Shall we proceed on the principle of isola-tion, ever trying to protect ourselves from exposure to possible suffering? The Stoics said in substance, "Don't love your wife or child too much, and then you will not be bowled over by their loss." Shall we keep ourselves to ourselves and thus reduce the areas where we can be hurt? The trouble here is that when we shrink from possible pain, we find life shrink-

ing. Henry Link, writing as a psychologist, tells of a young
woman who came to him complaining that her circle of friendship was shrinking into shadowy loneliness. Delving into her
case history, Link discovered that she had grown up in a comfortable home, but that she had never put herself out to mingle
with people she did not think she would enjoy. When company came who did not appeal to her, she simply kept to her
room. Thus never putting herself out for others, she found
herself progressively left out by others.

The person who would avoid discomfort by keeping to
himself must do so because he loves himself. Yet, strangely
enough, such persons do not like to be left alone with themselves. The self-centered individual is no better company for
himself than he is for others.

Is there any hell worse than that of being undisturbed? One
who was once a man of affairs, active in his community, suffered such reverses that he came to New York City "down
and out." Recently he said: "Try to imagine what it's like
never to have a phone call, never to receive a letter, never to
have anyone ask for you. It's hell." That man's loneliness, it
would seem, resulted from no fault of his own. But the person who keeps himself to himself, seeking to avoid all risk of
discomfort or sorrow, is headed for the hell of loneliness.

Swinburne, so far as his biography reveals, was never beset
by any very tragic troubles. He had his disappointments, to
be sure. He suffered some professional criticism. But he was
the scion of comfort and culture. He was sufficiently a devo-
tee of the carefree life to aim his shafts of scorn at Christianity
as being too somber. He referred to Jesus as "the pale Galilean," whose frosty breath killed the gay flowers of Greek
culture. Yet with all his pursuit of life's pleasantness, Swinburne revealed his weariness of living:

From too much love of living,
From hope and fear set free,
We thank with brief thanksgiving
Whatever gods may be
That no life lives forever;
That dead men rise up never;
That even the weariest river
Winds somewhere safe to sea.

On the other hand, those who mourn for the sufferings of others, those who enter into the sorrows of others, those who "bear one another's burdens and thus fulfill the law of Christ," such persons do expose themselves to pain, for the more they love the more they suffer; but they also find healing through their efforts to heal the hurts of others. All true happiness contains pain as a smothered element.

When John Bright lost his lovely young wife, his friend Richard Cobden came to comfort him in his blinding grief. Cobden told Bright about the thousands of British homes which were in the shadow of hunger because of the Corn Laws, and challenged the brilliant statesman to go out and help relieve the suffering. In going forth to lift the burdens of others, John Bright found solace in his own sorrow.

There is a reason why the darkness of sorrow deepens our affection for one another. The reason is that we are both more lovable and more loving when sorrow softens us. When a man is riding high in unbroken success, we may admire and applaud him, yet feel little affection for him. But when adversity knocks him off his high horse, and he picks himself up, mellowed in spirit, courageously showing that he can take it, then our admiration is enriched by affection. The man is more lovable.

Also we are more loving when trouble calls forth our sacrifice. Love finds its deepest satisfaction in serving the object of its love. That is why a mother may often seem to love the black sheep of the family more than the others. She feels that he needs her more. A professional woman in Baltimore is doing a very noble thing for a helpless friend with whom she lives. In the morning she rises early enough to arrange the household before she leaves for her long hours of work. In the evening, she gives herself to getting the dinner and being a companion. Does she feel it to be a hardship? Quite the reverse. Her face is radiant at the thought that she can serve one who had befriended her in years past. Ah more, the very nature of love is such that she is finding its deepest satisfaction, the fulfillment of the need to be needed.

Or take our larger circles of fellowship, the Church for instance. What held the early Church together? The suffering and persecution. Its love feasts were held "amid an encircling gloom." When the members left their places of meeting, they went forth knowing the dangers they risked. If the early Church had been run on the principle of self-interest, it would never have survived. The Christian Church has outlived all secular organizations because, by and large, it has been a fellowship of the serving and the suffering.

If we want the abundant life which Christ came to give, we must enter into "the fellowship of his sufferings." Our sympathies, like his, must get under the loads of burdened lives. As George Adam Smith said, Jesus was " 'the man of sorrows' because he felt all the sin of man with all the conscience of God." Yet with the weight of the world's sorrow in his heart and the shadow of the cross athwart his face, he could say to his followers: "In the world ye shall have tribulation: but be of good cheer; I have overcome the world." Christlike compassion finds comfort through the sorrows it shares.

STRENGTH THROUGH SORROW

In his "Seven Lamps of Architecture" John Ruskin maintained that the element of shadow adds to the ruggedness and strength of a structure. A towering wall which casts a shadow, or a deep penetrating recess which holds a shadow—these give an impression of strength not conveyed by sunny smoothness. So in life, when we read a biography, we find those chapters most gripping which show how this person came through the dark places of his career. When a man can live through tragedy, deeply lined of face perhaps, but not dimmed of eye or broken in spirit, he takes on something of the majesty of manhood.

Some years ago Edna Ferber in her book *So Big* portrayed a magnificent pioneer woman. Through struggle and sacrifice, this woman had surmounted obstacles and worked her way up to a place of influence and affluence. She had developed a strong, integrated personality. But she had a son who grew up in the shelter of success. He chose the easiest paths. He lived in the soft circles of city life. He achieved little; his character was less. One day the mother took a good look at her handsome, feckless son, so suave, so polished, yet so pliable. Sadly she said, "You're just too smooth."

When one visits the palace at Versailles, he is shown the spot where Louis XIV was wont to sit and listen to his court preachers. That proud monarch, despite the extravagant worldliness of his court and his own personal irregularities, was a connoisseur of good preaching. He wanted "all this, and heaven too." He desired the consolations of religion without undergoing its cleansing. One of the greatest of his court preachers, Massillon, on a certain occasion delivered before Louis a sermon containing these words:

If the world addressed your majesty from this place, the world would not say, "Blessed are they that mourn," but "Blessed is the prince who has never fought but to conquer; who has filled the universe with his name; who through the whole course of a long and flourishing reign enjoys in splendor all that men admire— extent of conquest, the esteem of enemies, the love of his people, the wisdom of his laws." But, sire, the language of the gospel is not the language of the world.

Truly the language of the gospel does run counter to the world's idea of happy and successful living. But judged by its fruits, which is the more satisfying, the life which is never ploughed by affliction or harrowed by sorrow and grows up a weedy patch of lush appetites, or the life that is mellowed by some misfortunes, subdued by some disappointments, and deepened by some suffering?

Contrast the portrait of Louis XIV, fleshy and somewhat sensual of face, with the lean lined features of the sad-eyed Lincoln. And then recall what Stephen Benet interprets Lincoln as saying:

> O Will of God,
> I am a patient man, and I can wait
> Like an old gunflint buried in the ground
> While the slow years pile up like moldering leaves
> Above me, underneath the rake of Time.
>
> .   .   .   .
>
> That is my only virtue as I see it,
> Ability to wait and hold my own
> And keep my own resolves once they are made

In spite of what the smarter people say.
I can't be smart the way that they are smart.
I've known that since I was an ugly child.
It teaches you—to be an ugly child.

Watch the face of some friend as he comes through great tribulation. At first, he may look as if drained of his very life-blood. But into his eyes there comes a look of deepened sympathy, into his strength a new quietness, into his whole bearing a new refinement. Such persons are the ones to whom others go for solace.

The late Dr. Ray Allen of Buffalo was wont to translate the second Beatitude thus: "Blessed are they that mourn: for they shall be comforters." And in this he was true to apostolic usage, for Saint Paul writes of the "Father of mercies, and the God of all comfort; who comforteth us in all our tribulation, that we may be able to comfort them which are in any trouble."

No Sadness of Farewell

No promise of comfort would approach satisfaction if it evaded the fact of death, for "the last enemy that shall be destroyed is death." The Christian attitude of faith by which to secure comfort in the face of death is best expressed in a Beatitude which appears in the Fourth Gospel. After Thomas has been convinced, the risen Christ is reported as saying, "Blessed are they that have not seen, and yet have believed."

The belief in a life beyond has persisted through all ages, practically universal in all races. This conviction is strongest at our best moments, and rises out of our noblest emotion, that of love. It seems to involve the very integrity of the universe itself. The Creator has endowed us with the power to love, to evaluate, to hope. These powers are as integral to human nature as the hunger of the body or the air we breathe. Certainly the Creator who keeps faith with the cravings of our bodily instincts will not play false to the other half of our natures. Surely the Creator, who guides through the boundless sky the path of the migrating bird on its unerring flight, has not planted in man a migrating instinct only to mislead him when he sets out for the larger home of his soul.

If life ended at the grave, this would seem an irrational world. We should then have to believe that the universe, having groaned in travail to bring forth its highest creation, human personality, having nurtured this human being with parental care, having rounded him into maturity and enriched him with grace, then after all that infinite labor throws him on the dust heap, a piece of rotting flesh, less valuable than rusting iron, which can be salvaged for future use. We should have to believe that the genius of Beethoven composing a Ninth Symphony, or the spirit of Francis of Assisi leavening with love the sodden life of the Middle Ages, or the personality of Paul is of no more value than the leaves which go flying down the street before the autumn wind, "cast as rubbish to the void."

Our belief in immortality rests on the very integrity of the universe itself. But Christ enhances our belief in the fidelity of this world's government. In his view, this is our Father's world, a world that clothes the grass of the field, and feeds the fowl of the air, a world wherein earthly fathers give good things to their children, and our heavenly Father gives even so much better things to those who love him. As we catch the spirit of Christ's integrity, we feel covinced that we can trust him when he says about this hope of a life beyond: "If it were not so, I would have told you. I go to prepare a place for you." We add the conviction of Christ's integrity to our belief in the world's integrity. We could believe in immortality, even if the career of Jesus had ended at the Cross.

But the record of Christ did not end on Calvary. The stories of the Resurrection present difficulties. When, however, we let our minds lie open to the record and allow each Gospel to bring its wave of testimony in on our thought, we feel a rising tide of conviction in the truth of Christ's triumph over the grave.

The sadhearted women going out in the misty morning to anoint the body of their departed leader; the experience in the garden which sent them rushing back to bring the disciples; the evening walk to Emmaus, when a mysterious presence seemed to accompany them and to make their "hearts burn" within them on the way; the Upper Room a week later, with the disciples gathered about the still-doubting Thomas, and then his cry of conviction, "My Lord and my God,"— these Easter reports are told with such reticence and artlessness that we cannot believe they were inventions. If not invented, may these Resurrection reports constitute just another ghost story to be added to the world's collection? But what ghost ever had the effect of producing moral grandeur in the people who thought they saw him? When did a ghost drive men from abject terror to flaming courage? Yet that is what the Resurrection did for the disciples. It transformed them from defeated refugees, trying to slip out of Jerusalem's back streets, into triumphant, radiant apostles proclaiming the risen Lord.

Something happened which made Jesus more powerful on the streets of Jerusalem at Pentecost than he was on Palm Sunday. Was it all a delusion or illusion? Well, a false report might last a few days or months, but the Church which was founded on this report of the risen Christ has continued and grown through nineteen centuries, producing by its gospel the noblest characters known to history. If you can believe that a religious movement, founded on a falsehood, can produce men of integrity and go on growing until it numbers over 600,000,000 followers, then you are welcome to your opinion. But I find it harder to explain away than to explain.

The Resurrection account recalls by suggestion an experience of my school days. As a lad of thirteen I was accustomed to ride a horse three miles to school. One spring the heavy rains had raised the waters of the stream which I had to ford. As I approached the crossing in the deepening dusk I observed fresh tracks which revealed that others had been crossing there. No one, however, was in sight and I hesitated to urge my horse into the muddied rushing waters. Then suddenly a door opened in a farmhouse which stood near the opposite bank. From that open door a path of light fell across the swollen stream. In that light I took courage and rode my horse across. Similarly, the river of death is a turgid stream whose bottom and farther bank I cannot see. I do see tracks which make me think others must have gotten over. Socrates, drinking the hemlock for the sake of an ideal—certainly such a noble spirit could not have been deceived. Joan of Arc, led to martyrdom by her sense of divine duty—certainly the universe could not be so cruel as to crush the dreams of so pure a girl. Such lives have left intimations which lead me to think the river of death can be crossed. But the Easter Event is like the opening of a friendly door on the other side. It sheds a light on that crossing, and that light gives me confidence to face the future.

Yes, Christ has brought life and immortality to light through the gospel. That is the conviction which has carried the Christian movement for nineteen centuries.

But death is not swallowed up in victory unless we conquer

the *fear* of death, as well as the *fact* of death. The Grim Reaper has his victories this side of the grave.

Why are we afraid of death? Is it because we are loath to look death in the face? We are ever fleeing from death and casting frightened glances over our shoulder at the stern specter which dogs our steps. Perhaps this is partly the cause of our fear, for persons who have looked death in the face through some dangerous experience or some nearly fatal sickness do have a kind of calm courage. Certainly we see that it is not the actual physical pain of dying which makes it frightening, for our observation of death leads us to believe that the bodily anguish at the end is far less than many of the pains from which we recover. When Browning described the death of a loved one by saying, "God took her to Himself, as you would lift a sleeping child from a dark weary bed into your arms," he was picturing the gentleness with which the spirit so often slips out of the body.

No, it is not the pain of passing which makes the dread of death. Is it not rather the loss of the things we love, the leaving of something we have known for something strange? To assuage that sense of severance Christ gives us victory over the fear of death by turning our thoughts to the eternal and the invisible. When we abide in the thoughts of these until they abide in us, then we feel the joyous confidence of the late Robert Freeman:

> When souls go down to the sea by ship,
> And the dark ship's name is Death,
> Why mourn and wail at the vanishing sail?
> Though outward bound, God's world is round,
> And only a ship is Death.

When I go down to the sea by ship,
And Death unfurls her sail,
Weep not for me, for there will be
A living host on another coast
To beckon and cry, "All hail!"

III. The Most Misunderstood Virtue

Blessed are the meek:
for they shall inherit the earth.

IF WE WERE asked to make a list of the most essential
virtues, what would we include? Socrates held that there
is only one fundamental virtue, namely wisdom. In his opinion,
if a person knew the secret of his true welfare, he would be
sure to follow it, because everyone wishes his own good. Experience, however, has demonstrated the limitation of truth
in the old saying, "Knowledge is power." As Portia remarked
to her maid, "If to do were as easy as to know what were good
to do, chapels had been churches and poor man's cottages
princes' palaces."

The Greek thinkers, who followed Socrates, listed four
cardinal virtues: wisdom, courage, temperance, and justice.
When Jesus came, he took these Greek virtues for granted, but
gave them new depth and dimension. And then he added to
the list, making Christian ethics more sensitive and social.

Hence when the wise and experienced veteran Paul writes
to young Timothy, he counsels him, in the sixth chapter of
his first letter, to follow after six virtues. He lists them thus:
righteousness, godliness, faith, love, patience. These five we
would all put in our lists, would we not? But now the sixth
is the puzzler. It is meekness. Do we ever admire or applaud
or congratulate a man for his meekness? It might be said
that we seldom have a chance.

When we wish to describe meekness, we use certain anal-

61

ogies. We say, "He is as meek as a mouse." The expression conjures up the thought of shy, frightened souls, scurrying around in the corners of life, trying to get out of our way and usually succeeding in getting under our feet. Mice are not attractive to us. Neither are the "meek," as we commonly think of them.

Perhaps less opprobrium is cast by another colloquialism, "meek as a lamb." Lambs are lovable, but we are prone to pity them for their helplessness. Not many of us like to be thought of as sheep, either "lost" or found.

Dickens created a character who epitomizes the popular idea of meekness. The mental picture of Uriah Heep stirs our distaste and also our distrust. With his oily, smirking, bowing manner, he masked a really wolfish greed under an obsequious sheepishness. We think of him with eyes downcast, but looking out of their corners to turn a sharp trick.

The current concept of meekness runs directly counter to our ideas of successful, happy living. We admire strength. We teach our children to have self-assurance, to assert their rights and not let others run over them. We feel that unless we stand up for ourselves we shall be crowded out. Some years ago a British periodical in a spirit of irony offered a framed copy of this Beatitude to any meek person who had "made good."

The meek, we cynically admit, may get to heaven and be happy there, but they cannot expect to have anything in this world. And yet strangely enough, it is in this world, Jesus says, that they will get their reward. "Blessed are the meek: for they shall inherit the earth."

The Beginning of Meekness

We are born into a universe which is already created. We cannot demand of God that he make over this physical universe to suit our taste, as we might ask a landlord to do over an apartment to fit our desires. The shape of this earth is round. The canopy over it is prevailingly blue in color. If we do not like the earth's roundness and the sky's blueness—well, that is just too bad!

And in this universe there appear to be laws of the spirit quite as inexorable as those of the material realm. If we keep sowing a bad indulgence, we reap a habit. And if we keep sowing a habit, we reap a character. We cannot change the law of the harvest, that "whatsoever a man soweth, that shall he also reap." This realm into which we are born has a constitution, and whether we like it or not, we have to live under it. We cannot amend God's by-laws.

Into such a world we come as self-willed little creatures. We want what we want when we want it. Left to ourselves as infants, we would quickly destroy ourselves. A year-old child cannot be left alone in a room with an open fire. It would burn itself to death. It cannot be left alone in a yard where there is an open pool. It would drown itself. If the infant is to play safely, it must be put into a playpen. If it is to sleep safely, it must be put into a crib. The frames of the crib and playpen seem prison bars to the child, but they are necessary to teach it how to live under the constitution of its sphere.

When the child grows to adulthood, he may childishly feel that he can run away from the world's responsibilities. If so, he becomes a moral drifter and vagabond, begging his morsels of satisfaction at the back doors of life. The moral tramp drags his miserable existence to its close, "unwept, unhonored, and unsung."

Or he may defy the divine constitution of the moral universe, run counter to the established ethical codes, and risk whatever retribution such a course entails. That was the attitude of Satan, the prince of the fallen angels, as pictured by Milton. When he has been banished from heaven by the God whom he has defied, Lucifer surveys his new home in hell and declares:

> Here at least
> We shall be free; the Almighty hath not built
> Here for his envy, will not drive us hence:
> Here we may reign secure; and, in my choice
> To reign is worth ambition, though in Hell:
> Better to reign in Hell than serve in Heaven.

If one is determined to defy God and have his own way regardless of what happens, he may seem to do so for a time, but eventually he finds that his is a kingdom of hell.

Or one can look upon this world as a prison, feel himself chained by its restrictions, beat his hands against the bars until his spirit is broken. We know persons with a broken spirit. Their confidence has been crushed out of them; they know not what to trust; they have not the courage to call their souls their own. That is not meekness, though we may often call it so.

If, however, we do not run from the world's responsibilities like a moral tramp, or defy God like Milton's Satan, or become frustrated and fearful, but accept the world as God's school for developing souls and submit ourselves to his discipline, then we are on the way to discovering what the Bible calls meekness. We see what the prophet Micah saw, that God is not a whimsical despot who can be bought off by sacrificing thousands of rams and pouring out rivers of oil on the altar, but is a being who requires that we "do justly, love mercy and walk humbly" with him.

Then if we go on in the spirit of the thirty-seventh psalm we learn to fret not ourselves because of evildoers nor to be envious against the workers of iniquity. Instead of bruising our minds, beating against the bars of our limitations, we "trust in the Lord, and do good." If we keep such patient trust, the psalmist says we shall find that the evildoers shall be cut off and "the meek shall inherit the earth." Now we are beginning to catch the divine idea of meekness.

We follow the Scripture further. There came into the world one Jesus of Nazareth. Possessed of power amazing and immeasurable, he yielded his will completely to his heavenly Father. Having thus yoked himself to God, Jesus called to his fellow countrymen, saying: "Come unto me, all ye that labor and are heavy laden, and I will give you rest. Take my yoke upon you, and learn of me; for I am meek and lowly in heart: and ye shall find rest to your souls. For my yoke is easy, and my burden is light." There we have the last lesson in meekness. We are to begin by walking humbly with God, then learn not to fret ourselves because evildoers may seem to pass us, and then to yoke ourselves with God as did Christ in serving others. Meekness, as taught in Christ's school, is submission to God's mastery.

WHO ARE THE MEEK?

There is no single English word which precisely expresses the biblical idea back of the word translated "meek." The psalmist, after telling his people not to fret themselves because of the seeming prosperity of the wicked, assures them that "the meek shall inherit the earth." The Hebrew word used connotes "being molded." The meek are the God-molded, those who have submitted to the divine will, those who are patterned after God's purpose. The pushing arrogant evil-

doers may seem to succeed, but those whose minds are surrendered to the Lord will eventually occupy the land where
the wicked once were. So says the psalmist.

Consider Moses, the character other than Jesus whom the
Scripture specifically calls meek. Moses was no weak, anemic
creature by nature. He was a man of such fiery passions that
in his youth he slew an Egyptian in a fit of anger. Then Moses
took himself in hand by putting himself in God's hand. He
served God and his countrymen in those long years of struggle in the wilderness. When we turn to the twelfth chapter
of Numbers, we find Moses confronted by a threatened in-
surrection led by Miriam and Aaron. And the record is, "The
man Moses was very meek, above all the men which were upon
the face of the earth." Through long discipline he brought
his fiery passions under cool control. He had achieved what
Michelangelo depicts in the famous statue of Moses in the
Church of San Pietro in Vincoli at Rome, where we see the
marvelous repose concealing the sleeping thunder of Sinai.

Meekness is not apathy, or lack of spirit, or weakness, or
timidity. It is power blended with gentleness. It is the soul in
the majesty of self-possession, lifted above impulsiveness and
irascibility. It is that high and radiant state of mind in which
all the faculties function under the sway of their divine Master. Meekness is, as Henry Ward Beecher said, "the best side
of a man under provocation maintaining itself in the best
mood."

When the New Testament comes to state the Beatitude, it
uses a Greek word, "praos," which suggests the taming of
wild animals. The meek are the God-tamed. Just as a wild
horse is caught, haltered, and bridled, so man's wild nature
may be tamed by God. We think of Saul of Tarsus, rushing
around Palestine like a wild animal, raging against the new

Christian sect. He was fairly snorting in his anger. Then one day on the road to Damascus, Saul was corralled of God, thrown to the ground. And he heard a voice saying, "Saul, Saul, why persecutest thou me? . . . It is hard for thee to kick against the pricks." And that was the beginning of Saul's taming, until he who had been "breathing out fire and slaughter," as the record puts it, was transformed into an apostle, "fervent in spirit, serving the Lord." He became meek in the sense of being God-tamed.

When the French take up this Beatitude, their New Testament has a very interesting version, "Blessed are the debonair." That word at first glance suggests a most striking contrast to the drooping, spiritless creatures commonly thought of as the meek. We think of debonair people as gay, carefree, lighthearted. The translation does seem a bit too light, doesn't it? But the Gallic mind usually has a logic which cannot be easily dismissed. And in this case it is pointing toward a basic aspect of meekness. The meek man is God-trained. His strength is disciplined into such gentleness that he is one of God's gentlemen, carrying his virtues with easy grace, tossing off insults and slights with gay indifference, because he feels himself above the reach of petty rancor, and he refuses to be burdened by carrying grudges. He has the debonair attitude of one who is sustained by his own gentlemanliness, and feels that others at heart must be gentlemen.

Luther in translating this Beatitude uses a German word which means sweet-tempered. The meek are not only God-molded, God-tamed, God-trained, but God-tempered.

Temper is a curious but essential element in human nature. If we lose our temper, that's bad. If we show our temper, that's bad. Temper must be kept, but in the right proportion. To be God-tempered is to be conditioned somewhat as crude iron is treated in order to be transformed into steel.

This tempering process is to be seen in a person like the prophet Elijah. On Mount Carmel, battling against the priests of Baal, Elijah was a crude bludgeon. Then he became cold and inert, sitting under his juniper tree and bemoaning his lot, asking that God take away his life, because he was left alone to battle against evil. God thereupon sent him forth into the mountain, where the lightning flashed and the wind roared, but Elijah did not find God in these noisy elements. Then came the still small voice, and after that Elijah learned that "not by might, nor by power, but my spirit, saith the Lord of hosts." And he was tempered into God's effective tool, strong and flexible like fine steel.

Strength at Its Strongest

The bull in the china shop smashing the beautiful objects of art has strength—the strength of a bull. The bully in the crowd elbowing his way to the front and bowling over his weaker brethren has strength—the strength of a bully. But the Servant of the Lord, the divine Deliverer, who so restrains himself that he does not break the bruised reed, has a superior strength —the strength of God. So says Isaiah.

God has power which is manifest in spectacular ways. We hear this same prophet speak of God holding "the nations as a drop in the bucket" and taking up "the isles as a very little thing." But when God brings his power to supreme demonstration, he does so by restraint. Power held in restraint is power at its highest, for then is shown not only the possession of strength but also the possession of the power to control the strength one possesses.

When we stand before a mighty waterfall, a majestic mountain, a roaring volcano, we are awed by the power of God.

But when Jesus sought to impress his hearers with divine power at its best, he bade them consider the fowls of the air, the lilies of the field, the little child in their midst. When God's power restrains itself to touch the lily to pure whiteness, to care for the falling sparrow, to flush the cheek of a child with the blush of innocence, then divine strength is demonstrated in its highest form. As Alfred North Whitehead says, "The image under which the nature of God can best be conceived is that of a tender care that nothing be lost."

When Martin Luther was a young man, a comrade at his side was struck by lightning. The shock sobered young Luther and set him seeking for God. But the lightning flash did not reveal to Luther the God he was seeking. That revelation came to Luther through reading about a tender, merciful God who "was in Christ reconciling the world unto himself," a loving Father who goes out to meet a prodigal and justifies him by faith.

Likewise, the strength of God's servants is at its highest when restrained to gentleness. Ruskin took pains to point out that fineness of nature and delicate sensibilities are the marks of a gentleman, and that they are compatible with heroic strength. In fact, says Ruskin, heroic strength is not conceivable without such delicacy. Second thought should remind us that it takes strength to be gentle. It is an error to think that gentleness is the mere absence of vigor. Weakness totters and tugs at its burden. In Walter Scott's *Ivanhoe* the dwarf who attended the knight at the tournament tried to lift the bleeding sufferer. His weakness made him stumble and caused the knight intense pain. When the giant of the strong arm came, he lifted the unconscious sufferer like a feather's weight, and without a jar bore him away to a secure hiding place for healing and recovery.

When we study the truly great characters of history, we see that gentleness was the test of their gianthood and fine considerateness was the measure of their manhood. Supreme in this regard stands Jesus of Nazareth. We speak of "the gentle Jesus." We portray him as the tender shepherd holding lambs in his bosom. When he was struck, he did not strike back. Many mistake his gentleness for weakness. But not so. It was the gentleness of power under superb control.

In his wilderness temptation at the start of his ministry, Jesus settled certain points about the use of his power. He would not use it for mere material benefits or spectacular demonstration or political rule. In accord with these principles Jesus restrained his power when he might have defied his critics and his crucifiers. Of course, Pilate and his cohorts and the crowd thought it was weakness on Jesus' part. But the writer of the Fourth Gospel saw into the secret of Jesus' restraint and interprets our Lord as saying: "I lay down my life, that I might take it again. No man taketh it from me, but I lay it down of myself. I have power to lay it down, and I have power to take it again."

It took quite a while for even his closest followers to understand why Jesus allowed himself to be crucified when he might have avoided it. But understanding eventually broke on their minds, and Paul went forth to preach Christ crucified as "the power of God and the wisdom of God."

It is hard for us of the power era to appreciate that gentleness is the mark of gianthood. We live and move and have our being in an atmosphere of mechanical power. We measure our machines by their horsepower, our men by their money power, our nations by their military power. And when we turn in this high-powered age to talk about the power of God showing itself at its best in the restraint which would not break a bruised reed, it sounds to many like such stuff as dreams are made on—and sermons!

What Do the Meek Get?

The meek are blessed because they get more values out of themselves. As Gerald Heard suggests, this God-taming does for man's nature something like that which domestication has done for a branch of the wolf family. The dog, as we know, is kin to the wolf. Through creative love the wolfish nature has been tamed and his temper has been changed to trust, until the dog has become the companion of man. The dog, moving around with his master, enjoys really more freedom than the fear-haunted wolf; he enters into the larger interests of the household; in short he finds a fullness of life denied to the wolf. Instead of being weakened, his courage is increased. The wolf, like most other wild animals, is a natural coward, the slave of fear; but the dog guarding his master or his house is self-forgetfully brave.

If we wish to bring this analogy of the wolf-dog relationship closer home, we might think of those human beings whom we call "wolves" prowling around our streets and taverns, preying upon the objects of their lustful desires. With all their love "affairs" and transient conquests, the human wolves do not get a fraction of the lasting satisfaction found by those men who faithfully submit to the loyalties and disciplines of family life. As the former grow older, the shadows of insecurity deepen and the stolen pleasures pall, until their wolfish spirits wail toward exhaustion on life's dreary wastes.

Yes, to be tamed and trained of God, as the meek are, gives freer use of one's native powers. The meek get more values out of themselves because their passions are under control and not ever beating against the bars, using up energy which might be otherwise used. Having themselves well in hand, they can put their hands to more things.

The meek also get more values out of themselves because their anger is under better restraint and they are not ever having those experiences which as we say "just burn us up." Queen Elizabeth, who knew something about hot temper, once said to a courtier who had lost his head, "Ah, Sir Philip, anger often makes men witty but it always keeps them poor."

Moreover, the meek have their ambitions as well as their anger under such control that they are not made restless by frustrated desires and wounded vanity.

And most of all they get more satisfaction because they are trying to get the values out of themselves rather than into themselves. The selfish, proud person who seeks to crowd things into his life has a limit to his capacity. But the meek unselfish soul who seeks to pour himself out for others finds in himself an artesian "well of water springing up into everlasting life."

Secondly, the meek are blessed because they get not only more out of themselves, but also more values out of others. The selfish individualist may be ever so talented and yet fail to secure the co-operation of others. Such a man never builds up an organization or rallies others around him. The God-trained person is disciplined to work with others.

Daniel Frohman, reminiscing about the stage as he knew it in his long career, told of a dramatic incident in which the actress Modjeska figured. At the climax of one of her scenes, the curtain failed to come down. It was most embarrassing. The troupe thought, of course, that she would be furious at the stage hand responsible. But when she did meet the discomfited fellow a few moments later, she simply said,

"Naughty, naughty." Thereafter she had the whole company with her, body and soul.

Furthermore, the meek get the most values out of others because they enter into the joys of others. Not being envious, they rejoice in the successes of others. Thus they live expansively, multiplying their own lives in the careers around them.

The God-trained and God-tempered meek also get more values out of the objects around them. Yonder is a farmer who has lived on his land, husbanded his soil, watched it grow richer, lovingly tended his stock and his crops. In a way, he has given himself to his farm. He dies. His son in Chicago or Denver inherits the farm. He holds legal title to it. He may receive rent from it. But does he get the same value out of that farm as did his father who put his life into it and developed it?

Or consider a man who loves and appreciates art. He collects pictures and lives with them, enriching his mind by companionship with their beauty. He passes away, and his son inherits the collection. But the latter has no understanding of art. His legal ownership does not give him the values which his father enjoyed through giving himself to art.

Who get the more value out of things? The persons who hold title to them, or the persons who put life into them and thus appreciate them and use them? The latter, of course. Now, the God-trained men we call the meek get the value out of what they have, because they put life into what they have; they regard things appreciatively rather than possessively. They feel themselves stewards rather than owners, and thus they are concerned with possessions for the purpose of use rather than for pride and prestige. They think of themselves as heirs of God and joint-heirs with Jesus Christ. Hence they share the apostle's feeling when he said, "All [things] are

yours; and ye are Christ's; and Christ is God's." In short, the
meek are blessed because they get more out of life.

Still more can be said. When we submit to divine mastery
until we attain self-mastery, we get mastery over the circumstances around us. When we have ourselves well in hand,
we have so much more power for handling other things. When
we have our passions under control, we can be a steadying and
pacifying force in our family and community circles. We do
not say impulsive things which we shall regret next day.
When we have so mastered our energy that we do not spread
out in a splurge of self-importance, we generate power, which
in any sphere of life makes for leadership.

The man who is meek in the sense of being God-mastered
and self-mastered has a winsome and winning power. He
possesses what Milton called "the invincible might of meekness." He wins the hearts of men; and, remember, no defeat
of enemies by force, no conquest of territory, becomes a real
victory until it results in winning the response of men's minds
and hearts. When Hitler entered Paris with his triumphant
legions, he stood on the Trocadero and looked across the
beautiful city of Paris. With that sentimentality which he possessed blended with his cruelty, he said in emotional voice:
"Great city! I have conquered her by force; I will now conquer her by love." Of course, he never did. To overrun a
country with arms does not bring its people to your arms.
That is a truth which militarists and the advocates of force
overlook. People held against their will do not prove profitable
subjects or prospective friends.

The old proverb has the truth: "He that is slow to anger is
better than the mighty; and he that ruleth his spirit than he that
taketh a city." In the long run, the figures that most firmly
hold the hearts of men are the rulers of the spirit, like Socrates,

Confucius, Francis of Assisi, and far above all others, Jesus of Nazareth.

If worldly men remain too blind to believe this Beatitude, then, "Blessed are the meek: for they shall inherit the earth" after the proud have killed themselves off trying to possess it.

IV. Making Good Wishes Work

Blessed are they which do hunger and thirst
after righteousness: for they shall be filled.

WE HAVE a common saying that "the wish is father to the thought." We mean by this that the wish to have a thing so begets the belief that it is so. We might also coin a proverb that the wish is big brother to the will. Our wills follow our wishes around as little boys trail their big brothers.

If wishes are thus so powerful that they father our thoughts and lead our wills, does not the strategy of the good life suggest giving more attention to our wishes? That would seem to have been the method of Jesus. He did set men's wills to work. But even more, he set their wishes to work. In that Jesus showed himself a master Teacher.

Consider a schoolroom. There before the teacher is a class of pupils, each of whom is a bundle of desires. Some of those wishes are wholesome, some mischievous, perhaps even bad. If the teacher sets out primarily with the purpose of restraining the pupils' wayward desires, she is likely to find herself in a nest of porcupines whose pricks of irritation will make her life miserable. The good teacher is one who dissolves the problems of discipline by arousing new interests. The effective principle in teaching as in life generally is to overcome evil with good.

Evil is the absence of good as darkness is the absence of light. And just as darkness cannot be driven out of a room with a fan or sword but by turning on the light, so evil is banished by turning on goodness. Christ came as the Light of the world that men's eyes might be opened. To open the mind with good wishes is better than to grit the teeth against bad ones.

Jesus said, "I am the bread of life: he that cometh to me shall never hunger; and he that believeth on me shall never thirst." Our Lord was here speaking about the lower hungers of earth, by which the crowd had mistakenly been lured to follow him. When we feed our spirits on the bread of heaven which Christ came to bring, we are lifted above the physical cravings which fail to satisfy the hunger of the soul. The higher hunger drives out the lower.

Hunger That Means Health

Hunger and thirst are signs of health, as well as signals of need. When we are sufficiently "poor in spirit" to surmount our pride; when through mourning for our own sins and the sufferings of others, we find the keys of comfort and courage; when God has tempered us into the meekness which makes for efficient living, we get a taste of the good life which arouses our appetite for more. Hence the first three Beatitudes lead to the fourth: "Blessed are they which do hunger and thirst after righteousness: for they shall be filled."

A mother was riding on the train with her four children. She did not try to interest the little ones; she only sought to restrain them. Her conversation was a mere series of ejaculations: "No," "Stop," "Don't do that." One little fellow ran to the other end of the car beyond the mother's range of vision. She sent his older sister after him with the injunction, "Go see what Willie is doing, and tell him to stop it." She seemed to assume that everything they did was wrong; and in the atmosphere she created, the assumption was pretty nearly correct.

Contrast her conduct with that of a wise and patient mother. The latter restrains too, but she looks for the good points to encourage. She awakens wholesome interests. She banks on the best, and thereby she brings out the best. She gradually changes her children's attitude from fear of what she may do to hurt them to fear of what they may do to hurt her.

Jesus sought to arouse a hunger and thirst after righteousness. When we hear the words on his lips, we must try to feel their intensity. Do we know hunger as did the people of Palestine, who in Jesus' day lived close to the margin of malnutrition? One poor harvest and parents might hear their children cry for bread. Our Lord beheld the lean and hungry look of multitudes who lived a hand-to-mouth existence.

Sholem Asch, after World War I, wrote a significant book, entitled *Three Cities*, in which he depicted the devastation of eastern Europe. He told of a young man who left his comfortable home and went to work seeking to alleviate the conditions of the destitute. Despite all his sympathetic efforts, he felt a barrier between himself and those he sought to help. He could not understand this, until one day a voice from the crowd cried to him, "Have you ever been hungry?" One has to know the gnawing ache of hunger, one has to see the gaunt bodies of little children going hungry to bed, if he is to catch the full intensity of Jesus' words in this Beatitude.

And while hunger can be terrible, thirst can be far more so. It flogs the weary body with whips of flame. It mocks the desert traveler with the maddening mirage. His parched throat and burning lips become unable to frame words. And Palestine was a dry country as well as a starved one. The burning sands, the searing winds, the relentless sun beating down from a heaven of brass—all these are reflected in the many biblical references to springs and brooks and thirst.

When, therefore, we read Jesus' words, "Blessed are they which do hunger and thirst," we must try to catch the force of those longings as experienced in our Lord's land of scarcity on the edge of the desert. He is not describing a mere vague preference for "doing the right thing." He is not uttering a pious platitude, "Blessed are they who want to be good." He is depicting a longing which means the difference between life and death.

Gautama Buddha vowed that he would die in his tracks unless he could find the way of life, the path of deliverance. And the story is told that after he thought he had found the true way, a certain man came asking that he might be shown. Buddha led him down to the river. It was at bathing time, and the seeker assumed that he was to undergo a ritual of purification. When they were some distance out in the stream, Buddha suddenly grabbed the man and held his head under water. Finally, in a last gasp the fellow wrenched himself loose, and his head came above water. Quietly Buddha asked him, "When you thought you were drowning, what did you desire most?" The man gasped, "Air." Back came Buddha's reply, "When you want salvation as much as you wanted air, then you will get it."

No less urgent must be the desire for righteousness as depicted by Jesus. But hunger and thirst are not mere cravings of a critical moment, as is the gasp of a drowning man for air. They are recurring longings, calling for repeated satisfaction.

Some time ago after a train wreck in which several had been hurt and one killed, a fellow passenger, very much sobered by his near approach to death, said, "Believe me, I'm going to walk the straight and narrow from here on in." His good intentions were no doubt sincere at the moment of speaking; but good resolutions are not likely to be sustained merely by the memory of a miraculous escape from death. The jet propulsion of momentary gratitude does not of itself keep a person going Godward very long. Not by flashes of feeling, but by a hunger and thirst after righteousness are we filled with the food by which we grow in grace and goodness.

The persons who live for the things of this world show more shrewdness and do more long-range planning than religious folk do for their spiritual concerns. Look around and behold the ingenuity shown in devising new ways of doing business. Think of the inventiveness revealed in our industrial programs. Consider the energy given by evildoers to find ways of out-witting the law. And ponder the billions being appropriated by governments in order to surpass other nations in the arts of destruction. What skill, what smartness, what foresight are manifested by the children of this world in getting the things of this world.

When we contrast with all this the comparative complacen-cy and lack of up-to-dateness shown in the promotion of righteousness, we see the point of Jesus' statement, "The children of this world are in their generation wiser than the children of light." The children of light want a better world, but if it were a choice between that and a better place in the world as it is, they would choose the latter. They are in-terested in good causes, but most of them rather mildly so, and their financial support comes out of that fraction of their income which the government would take anyway in taxes. They perhaps belong to the church, for it is still rather a mark of respectability to have church connections, some connec-tions being considered more respectable than others. They devote some time to the service of the church and other or-ganizations of uplift, but they give usually only the fag-ends of their time and the snap-ends of their judgment, because their main business is to advance their own careers. They leave the burden of carrying on the church and the reform movements to professional workers, who are popularly considered of rather second-rate mentality, since it is assumed that all persons of first rank would go into more profitable lines of work.

Of course, there are many who really give their whole hearts and minds to advancing the kingdom of God. But by and large, is it not true that the service given to getting the world ahead is sluggish and slovenly and indifferent compared to the shrewdness devoted to getting ahead in the world? And Jesus in his parable of the unjust steward was calling the children of light, that is the good people, to bring their virtues up-to-date, to put more ingenuity and inventiveness into their goodness, in short to match the children of this world in resourcefulness and foresight.

Righteousness That Means Goodness

If virtue is to be brought up to vital effectiveness, the children of light must develop their good intentions into intelligent goodness.

Good intentions are basic to all goodness. Motives are at the heart of morals. "What did he mean to do?" is the question a parent must ask in appraising the conduct of a child. And that is the question a court must ask when a crime has been committed. Jesus, in measuring deeds, took into account their intent. When a grateful woman anointed his head and feet with an expensive perfume and the disciples rebuked her for this extravagance, he bade them let her alone, saying that she had wrought a good work. The Master valued that lavish show of love, because he looked upon the heart and saw the purity of motive.

Yet, fundamental as motives are, there is a saying, "Hell is paved with good intentions." About a century ago Jeremy Bentham and his followers in the so-called Utilitarian School were denouncing the cruelties and blunders of conscientious people. They observed the futility and harmfulness of so many good intentions and noble sentiments. The cure of all this, they believed, was to shift the focus of moral judgment from motives to results. They concluded that the one desirable end of all living was happiness, defined as pleasure and the absence of pain. Since all motives could be reduced to the desire for happiness, the terms "good" and "bad" do not apply to intentions at all, but only to methods and results. According to the Utilitarian philosophy, actions are good in proportion as they tend to promote happiness, and wrong if the result is the reverse.

Well, the Christian cannot follow such reasoning and say that a happy result is the sole measure of rightness in an act. Nor on the other hand can he go with those who say that the motive determines the goodness of a deed. The Christian has a moral duty to keep his eye on both his motives and the consequences of his conduct. He must study the situation in which his action will operate as well as scan the motives which move him to act. We have a moral obligation to be intelligent.

When Jesus was asked what is the first and great commandment, he replied, "Thou shalt love the Lord thy God with all thy heart, and with all thy soul, and with all thy mind." We are called to put our minds as well as our hearts into the service of God. It is not enough to say of a person that his heart is in the right place if his head and hands are in the wrong places.

When Jesus during his earthly career sent his disciples forth on a mission of healing and teaching, he said to them, "Be ye wise as serpents and harmless as doves." That was his figurative way of bidding them to use tact and wisdom. They were not to demean their divine calling by blundering methods. They were not to arouse needless antagonisms by doing the right things in the wrong way.

Again and again in the gospels, our Lord called his followers to use their heads as well as their hearts. He is summoning us now to put vitality and inventiveness into our virtues, to illumine the ageless qualities of kindness and generosity with imagination and insight, to bring the old commandments up to our new frontiers of temptation. "Thou shalt not steal" must have its points of application sharpened so that it pricks the conscience of the man who defrauds through a corporation as well as of the man who picks a pocket. The old injunction, "Thou shalt not bear false witness," must be brought up to date so that it stops a propagandist from falsifying facts as well as stops a man from lying about his neighbor.

Some years ago a doctor said to his minister, "Why should I go to church? I learned the Ten Commandments and a lot of Bible stories when I was a boy. Why do I need to go and hear all that stuff again?" Suppose he adopted the same attitude in his practice of surgery. Suppose he read no professional journals, attended no clinics, studied no books because he once went to medical school. We would not care to have such a backwoods surgeon operate on our backbone.

Moreover, if the children of light are to match the children of this world, they must develop their righteousness into goodness.

Righteousness, like good motives, is basic to morality. Righteousness is defined as conformity to the divine standard of right and justice. This divine standard needs ever to be kept in mind. Justice Harold McKinnon of San Francisco recently delivered a speech at a conference of federal judges. In it he shows that the trend of recent years has been to treat law as the mere creation of the state designed as an expedient for the good of the people. Such a flexible concept of law opens the way to all sorts of distortion. Justice McKinnon argues for the recognition of "the law of nature," the divine law which is basic and prior to statute law. Conformity to divine law, which is righteousness, is essential to virtue.

Nevertheless, when we speak of "a righteous person" does it sound quite so attractive as when we speak of "a good person"? Paul seems to feel the distinction when he writes to the Romans: "Scarcely for a righteous man will one die; yet peradventure for a good man some would even dare to die." What is the difference? Isn't it this: that the righteous person has his eye solely on the law which he is trying to keep, while the good person, as we call him, has his eye also on the other man whom he is trying to help?

Now, the Christian is called to keep his eye both on the law and the person. Jesus said, "Think not that I am come to destroy the law, or the prophets: I am not come to destroy, but to fulfill." He did not let go the divine law. But he also kept his eye on the people. Is that not wherein he differed basically from the scribes? They pored over the laws, to see that not one jot or tittle was broken; Jesus bent over broken bodies and wounded spirits to see that not one was overlooked. The Master so mixed righteousness with love that it became lovable goodness.

Have you ever been in a gathering where some person purses her lips, draws herself up in her indignant dignity, and says, "I hate to say it, but I feel it my duty to say it"; and then proceeds with evident delight to prick somebody's reputation with her rapier of gossip. Whenever a person begins by saying, "I feel it my duty to say," we should become a bit wary. People who do duty merely for the sake of duty never make it very attractive. We are helped by good deeds when they are pulled out by the love of people rather than pushed out by cold principles.

Take the story of the Samaritan on the Jericho Road. Suppose when he saw the wounded man, he had said: "Now I am a Samaritan, and not in very good standing in this Jewish region. Therefore I had better aid this poor victim." With that motive, it would have been the Story of the Respectable Samaritan, not worth much. Or suppose he had said to himself, "My religion teaches that it is a man's duty to help another in distress, and to do so will assure me merit in the Day of Judgment. Therefore I shall help this man left by the robbers." With that motive, the parable would have been the Story of the Righteous Samaritan, not very inspiring. But no, the Samaritan, forgetting himself, put the wounded man on his beast, took him to an inn, and bade the innkeeper care for him. This motive gives us the Story of the Good Samaritan. And human hearts have been stirred by it down the centuries. Why does that parable live? For the same reason that Christ lives in human hearts. It is righteousness redeemed by love into goodness.

Furthermore, if the children of light are to match the children of this world, they must develop their patterns of goodness into paths of goodness. In its elementary stages, the training of a child is pretty much a matter of copying patterns. The little child does what the mother does. It does not know why. It simply copies her. And when we say to a child, "Behave yourself," we rather imply that the more nearly it acts as we do the more we shall approve its behavior. But just to make children second editions of ourselves is not wise, for with most of us, one edition is enough for the world. Goodness begins as copying a pattern, but it must go on to become following a path, for no one of us is quite like any other and each of us must make his own way.

This was a point Jesus stressed. He told his followers that they were not to copy the Pharisees who kept the little patterns of respectable morality, that unless their righteousness exceeded the righteousness of the scribes and Pharisees they would not see the kingdom of heaven. The followers of Christ were to do something unusual, to go the second mile, to turn the other cheek, to get out of the groove. They were to take Christ's yoke upon them and learn of him. To be good means taking the road with Christ, ever going upward toward higher interests, ever outward toward larger, more unselfish concerns.

And in these paths of goodness, Christ gave flying goals. A man came asking Jesus to help him get a larger share of his family estate. Our Lord replied, "Who made me a judge or a divider over you?" And then the Master said to the onlookers, "Beware of covetousness." Suppose he had given a legal adjustment. As a pattern it would have been dated. But covetousness is just as current an issue today as it was then.

Another came to Jesus and asked if it were lawful to pay tribute to Caesar. The Master answered, "Render unto Caesar the things which be Caesar's, and unto God the things which be God's." Any specific tax regulation of that first century would not be of much help now; but the question of separation of church and state is one of the livest issues we face.

Again, Jesus was asked, "How oft shall my brother sin against me and I forgive him? Till seven times?" Jesus said unto him, "I say not unto thee, until seven times; but until seventy times seven." In love and forgiveness, the sky is the limit. As Professor Tillich says, love is one thing in life which can transform itself according to the concrete demands of every individual and social situation without losing its eternity and dignity and unconditional validity.

Christ gave us paths rather than patterns, and his paths lead toward the infinity of perfection. Christ gave us love to supplement our laws, and love is never repealed. Therefore he is "Jesus Christ, the same yesterday, and today, and forever."

THE FORMULA FOR FULFILLMENT

The soul's hunger for wholeness may be inarticulate. We may be like children crying in the night, "with no language but a cry." This longing for rightness may be vocal, yet vague. Out of his long campus experience, Dean Robert R. Wicks declares that the main difficulty with undergraduate religion is sheer vagueness.

When we leave our thinking at loose ends, it is so easy for our conduct to get caught in loose living. Unless we think our way through to some definite conclusions, unless we follow a line of thought through and tie it with a knot of convictions, our beliefs unravel into half-truths and our temptations assail us with those plausible clichés which the crowd takes for granted. Straight, clean living requires some straight, hard thinking about God and goodness. If we are troubled with doubts about God, then let us start with some convictions about the simple basic decencies. By keeping faith with the highest we know, we acquire faith in the highest we can know.

In A. J. Cronin's *The Keys of the Kingdom* there is a conversation between a young Scottish physician and a Roman Catholic priest. The young doctor, despite his earnest seeking for spiritual enlightenment, has never been quite convinced of God's existence. But he had gone out to China to help cure the plague which was raging. In his efforts to heal he contracted the disease and lay dying. As he gasped his last breaths, he said to the priest, "I still can't believe in God." The priest tenderly replied, "Does that matter now? He believes in you."

Of course it matters whether we can believe in God; it mattered desperately in the dying doctor's disturbed thinking. But when faith in God fails to come through, we can keep faith with God.

Jesus prescribed the formula by which the vague longing for the good life can be developed into the hunger and thirst that can be divinely filled. These are the steps: "Ask, and it shall be given you: seek and ye shall find; knock, and it shall be opened unto you."

By asking of God we show our need and receptivity. God cannot give to the self-sufficient and the unresponsive. "Woe unto you that are full! for ye shall hunger." But until they do hunger for the good life, God cannot give it unto them. The Father of the Prodigal yearns to give good things to his son yonder in the far country feeding himself among the swine, but not until the lad has left the swineherd and has come asking to be taken again into the Father's household can the latter fill the emptiness, which the husks of low indulgence could not long satisfy.

Moreover, when we ask, we clarify our wishes and needs. God knows what we have need of, but we often do not. We need to bring our unanalyzed sense of lack into focus by framing specific petitions. Truly, "Prayer is the soul's sincere desire, uttered or unexpressed." But Paul sees the need of being more concrete: "With the heart man believeth unto righteousness; and with the mouth confession is made unto salvation." When we phrase our needs in words, we fix them more clearly in our minds.

In the Lord's Prayer, the words, "Give us this day our daily bread," come trippingly from the tongue. But how much more effective would be our petition if we thought specifically what we are hungry for? It helps mightily to take a definite preview of the day's possible needs: The spiritual food we shall need at breakfast time to strengthen us for the burden of the day's tasks, the love we must have at noon if we are to be brotherly toward that business associate who is so trying, the moral courage we shall need tonight to fortify us against the temptations we shall face when the shadows bring out the wolfish instincts of the city's jungle.

And if our hunger and thirst after righteousness is to be filled we must be selective as well as specific in our asking. To that end Jesus gave us clear guidance: "Whatsoever ye shall ask in my name, that will I do, that the Father may be glorified." Some of our desires are too low to be asked "through Jesus Christ our Lord." The appetite for the fruit of indulgence by the eating of which sin came into the world must be lifted into a taste for the fruit of the spirit by which the longing for sin is lost. And "the fruit of the spirit is love, joy, peace, long-suffering, gentleness, goodness, faith, meekness, temperance." When we have learned to like the taste of these fruits, then our desires have become identical with our needs. And when we want what we ought to have, we enter into the higher happiness.

Bad tastes are easily acquired. We pick up cheap tunes on the street. When we let ourselves go with the crowd, we gravitate toward the vulgar. But the appreciation of great art or noble music requires time and much living with. If duty is to be developed into desire, we must be more than merely receptive. We must go the second mile in satisfying our hunger and thirst after righteousness: "Seek, and ye shall find."

Consider love, which is the basic element in goodness. Despite much romantic talk we do not often "fall in love" at first sight. A couple, now happily married for some twenty-five years, was asked how their romance started. It was at the wedding of the wife's brother that they first met. After telling this, the wife quickly added, "And I didn't like him at all when I first saw him." Most successful marriages do not result from sudden emotional surges which sweep men off their feet. Some of us had to run quite a long way before we captured the hearts of our life-comrades. We "make love" to those we marry. And certainly we have to "make love" if we are to beget good will with those beyond our intimate circles, because from the sidewalk they do not look lovable. We must seek "to love rather than to be loved," "to comfort rather than to be comforted," "to understand rather than to be understood."

One of the most beautiful invocations is that of William Bright: "Oh, Almighty God, from whom every good prayer cometh, and who pourest out on all who desire it the spirit of grace and supplication, deliver us, when we draw nigh to thee from coldness of heart and wanderings of mind, that with steadfast thought and kindled affections we may worship thee in spirit and in truth, through Jesus Christ our Lord."

When we go to church we enter rather cold of heart, made so by the week's work and news. We look around us at our fellow worshipers, and our thoughts wander off in all directions. We get little out of the service until we are delivered from that mood, and our mind is brought to focus steadfastly on the scripture, the prayers, the message, the hymns. Then, if we do pay attention with steadfast thought, our affections

begin to kindle. Our memory begins to glow with warming re-
minders of God's mercies through friends and kinsfolk,
through the good earth and the blessings of this free land, and
most of all through the life of our Lord Jesus Christ. Our
imagination begins to work, and the church service comes
alive until we feel a "Presence that disturbs us with the joy of
elevated thoughts."

It is by steadfast thought that we kindle affection. Paying
attention is the price of love. In some communities is heard
this expression for courtship: "John is paying attention to
Mary." He pays attention with his mind, gazing at her, thinking of her when she is not present. Then he pays her atten-
tions of courtesy. Thus his love mounts.

Divine love, like human love, yields its satisfactions only
to those who seek with the whole mind and heart. Keep thinking about God and about Christ until your imagination begins
to work. Let your mind dwell on the great biblical scenes until
the characters come to life.

As Shelley said, the great instrument of the moral good is
the imagination. When the imagination and the will are in
conflict, the imagination always wins. The pictures we hang
in our minds set our wishes to work and shape their product.
Suppose we do spend two, three, four, perhaps ten minutes
in prayer each day. And then all the rest of the time we are
thinking about our own interests. What chance are we giving
God to answer our prayers? The trouble with so much of our
praying is that we ask for God's gifts while we keep thinking
about ourselves.

Some af our popular books on prayer today treat it as if it
were as simple as switching on the electric light. Just ask God
for health and happiness, for peace of mind and prosperity, and
presto, it is done. Ah, it's not so simple. We must ask God; we

must also seek God, seek him through the places where he
has revealed himself, in the scenes of holy Scripture, in the
lives of saintly souls, in the quiet beauties of nature. Yes, that
takes time; but when prayer is treated as a time-saving device,
it never becomes a life-saving force .

In a little book, *How to Conquer Your Seven Deadly Enemies*, James Barrett listed these enemies as: fear, regret, greed,
ambition, laziness, self-pity, and death. He said the distinguishing mark of laziness is that it is the most agreeable of all
our enemies. Laziness can hang around the house and never
get on our nerves. In fact, it is so congenial and friendly that
we call it by pet names. Seldom do we call our laziness by its
own name. But laziness, by whatever name we call it, is an
enemy that keeps our wishes from working. However much
we may ask God, unless we seek him with our mind and heart
and soul and strength, we shall not find him or his answers to
our prayers. God gives his highest only to our utmost.

Ask—that opens the doors of our hearts and minds. Seek—
that puts us on the way to finding God. Now let us go on to
the third step in Jesus' formula for making wishes work:
"Knock, and it shall be opened unto you."

Sometimes it seems that God's door is closed to our requests.
When Luke records these words of Jesus, he links them in
his eleventh chapter with the parable of the importunate man
who had a friend drop in on him one night after a long journey.
Having no food to give his guest, the man went to the house of
his neighbor, knocked on the door at midnight and called,
"Friend, lend me three loaves." From within a sleepy voice
answered, "Trouble me not; the door is now shut, and my
children are with me in bed; I cannot rise and give thee." Yet
our Lord went on to say that because of the man's importunity,
the neighbor finally did give him all that he needed.

That parable, of course, is not designed to portray the nature of God, for God is never asleep nor reluctant to help. As the psalmist said, "He that keepeth Israel shall neither slumber nor sleep." The point of the parable is to teach the patience of seemingly unanswered prayer and the need of persevering in our petitions. Aye, more, in bringing our wishes to God, it sometimes happens that the divine door remains closed until we do something with our hands, as the man did who went and knocked.

One New Year's day, a minister's phone rang and a voice asked if interviews were ever granted on a holiday. The man came. He was very tense. His mother, to whom he had given himself, had passed away some six months before. He was not in financial distress, but he had no job, no interests, no friends. The ache of loneliness was like a terrific physical pressure. His mind was so distraught that he could not read or sleep. He was at dead center. He was consulting various persons, talking over and over his problems. But talk was not enough to get him off dead center. That man had to put his hand to something. He had to force himself to start doing something, however little, something which would get him out of himself.

"Seize the very first possible opportunity to act on every resolution you make and on every emotional prompting you may experience in the direction of the habits you aspire to gain. It is not in the moment of the forming but in the moment of their producing motor effects that resolves and aspirations communicate the new 'set' to the brain," says William James in his *Principles of Psychology*.

If the divine door does not seem to open, despite all your asking and seeking, do not give up in despair. Do not deny that there is a God or that he answers prayer. While you are waiting for God to answer your prayer, try to be an answer to somebody else's prayer. And while you are doing that, keep asking and seeking to find out whether you are part of your problem or part of the answer. Do something near at hand that you can do. Take hold of some task or duty that gives you a sense of reality.

"I know thy works: behold, I have set before thee an open door, and no man can shut it: for thou hast a little strength, and hast kept my word, and hast not denied my name."

Satisfying the Higher Hungers

To those who hunger and thirst after righteousness, the promise is, "they shall be filled." The words thus translated suggest "good grazing." They are reminiscent of the twenty-third psalm with its "green pastures" and "still waters."

Man hungers for more than the world can give. He "cannot live by bread alone." It is this higher hunger which distinguishes man from other animals. Carlyle suggested that man's distinguishing trait is that he is the only animal that cooks his food. The distinction, however, is in the food and not the mere cooking. Bernard Iddings Bell says, "Man is an animal which alone among the animals refuses to be satisfied by the fulfillment of animal desires."

Animal behavior, according to Dr. Bell, is the result of four urges: the hunger for food and drink, the hunger for rest, the hunger for play, and the hunger for sex. If under the last of these four hungers, Dr. Bell would include those urges which bind animals to their young and to the pack or flock, then we would agree that he has covered the roots of animal behavior. Allow the beast of the field to eat and drink his fill, to sleep when he is tired, to romp when he pleases, and to satisfy his procreative and gregarious urge, then that animal is content.

But not so with man. The prodigal in the far country of self-indulgence is not satisfied with the husks that the swine do eat. He is haunted by beyond-the-body hungers. Man must have more than enough to live *on*. He must have enough to live *for*.

Jesus taught that if we had enough to live for we would find enough to live on. That is what he meant, is it not, when he said: "Be not therefore anxious, saying, What shall we eat? or, What shall we drink? or Wherewithal shall we be clothed? ... For your heavenly Father knoweth that ye have need of all these things. But seek ye first his kingdom and his righteousness, and all these things shall be added unto you." This has always been a difficult statement for practical men to swallow.

Part of the difficulty, however, begins to dissolve as we realize that when we have much to live for, we do not seem to need so much to live on. Look at the young bride and groom, so deeply in love. They can be happy in the cheapest of apartments. Consider the scientist engrossed in some experiment. He almost forgets to eat. Recall how James M. Barrie found supreme delight when as a struggling young writer he lost himself in London working till the stars went out. When our minds are full of purpose, our lower hungers lose their pangs.

But if we are to have enough to live for, we need a purpose large enough to gather up our temporary interests into something which gives meaning and zest to the whole of life. Short-term purposes can keep us going for a while. A man may like his job so well that he never looks at the clock, but sooner or later he does look at the calendar and asks, "What is the use of it all? What does it all add up to?" We must enlist in causes larger and longer than our own lives, so that when age forces us to retire we can rejoice in the works which follow after us. Such is the satisfaction of those who hunger and thirst after righteousness. They see their lives adding up to a sum which is carried over into the next column of human figures. And being concerned for the Kingdom of God and his righteousness rather than for their own records, they are satisfied. As Woodrow Wilson is reported to have said about himself, they would rather fail in a cause that would eventually win than to win temporarily in a cause that would ultimately fail.

Reaching for high things which elude our grasp helps us to do better the things within our grasp. David desired to unite his people into a nation, to establish his capital at Jerusalem, and then to adorn that royal city with a temple to Jehovah. He never built the temple, but his aspiration toward the unattained helped him to reach better his other two goals. Curious paradox, but the hands that reach toward heaven are the ones most effective in the work of this world.

They who hunger and thirst after righteousness are filled with the satisfaction that they are in God's green pastures where the grazing is not limited. The fruits of the spirit are non-competetive possessions. The more others get of them, the more there are for us to enjoy. Hence if we think on the things that are true, honorable, lovely, and of good report, there need be no envious looking over the fences at greener pastures. When we seek righteousness rather than our rights, we find a contentment and peace of mind which the worldling cannot know.

Two brothers entered the ministry. One spent his life in an obscure New England village, growing gray in the service of his little flock. Although his name was not known outside his local community and his salary was most meager, he knew a happiness which was reflected in his benign and genial face. A statement of his lingers in my memory: "The only way a minister can be happy is to feel himself a channel."

The other brother rose to high ecclesiastical office. He was an impressive and pompous prelate. A view of him also remains etched on my mind. He was riding on a train from one speaking engagement to another. He was uneasy and dissatisfied. He complained that he had not been properly advertised in the city where he had just spoken, and he was fearful lest he be not properly prepared for at the next place. He hungered and thirsted after his own rights and power, and he was left empty of soul. His humbler brother hungered and thirsted after righteousness, and he was filled with contentment.

When we live for worldly ends, we shall never find satisfaction in this world. Moreover, if we live for the world's ends, we shall never find a satisfactory heaven, for if we are ever to live in the place Christ has prepared for his followers, we must learn here and now to like what Jesus called the "bread of heaven."

V. The Mystery of Mercy

Blessed are the merciful:
for they shall obtain mercy.

IF A POPULAR poll were taken as to which of the Beatitudes had the most appeal, the vote would probably be in favor of the fifth. The poor in spirit have to be explained before they are appreciated. Mourning wears a veil which has to be lifted before the blessing behind it can be seen. Meekness is so commonly misunderstood as weakness that many dismiss it without study. But when we come to talk about the merciful, there is a spontaneous appeal.

The word mercy summons images of a Good Samaritan helping a wounded man on the Jericho Road, of Red Cross nurses moving among sick soldiers, of kindly acts mingled even amid the cruelties of war, of generous deeds done by magnanimous natures. No characteristic brings us closer to our brothers than the trait of mercy. And when we think of God, the quality which makes him seem most lovable is his mercy.

Yet with all our praise of mercy, it is one of the most difficult of the virtues. Truly, kindness is the core of creation, but too superficial are those who would dismiss all discussion of creeds and say that all this old world needs is "the simple art of being kind." The trouble is that the art of being kind is not so simple. It calls for study, yes, and more!

What Is Mercy?

It would help us in understanding all the Beatitudes if we were to remember that Jesus took for granted the so-called cardinal virtues: justice, wisdom, temperance, and courage. He might have included in his list, "Blessed are the brave," or "Blessed are the just," but he assumed these. Jesus' teaching in the Beatitudes and in the whole Sermon on the Mount urges an ethic beyond the ordinary. He is ever asking, "What do ye more than others?" He insists, "Except your righteousness shall exceed the righteousness of the scribes and Pharisees, ye shall in no case enter into the kingdom of heaven." Hence when he says, "Blessed are the merciful," he is talking about a virtue beyond the ordinary.

Mercy begins in compassion and sympathy. The Good Samaritan pitied the poor roadside victim, but pity might have stopped there. No doubt the Levite as he passed by also felt sorry. Pity may shed tears of sympathy, but mercy takes action.

Moreover, mercy has a certain judicial element in its character. We may pity a person without passing judgment as to whether he deserves his suffering or punishment. But to be merciful means that we show compassion over and above what the sufferer or sinner deserves.

Thus mercy involves justice. Without the stabilizing element of justice, sympathy would be spineless and pity might play havoc. When a father, for instance, tries to be generous and forgiving without first trying to be just, he is likely to demoralize the character of his child. When a judge essays to dispense mercy without justice, he makes a mess of law and order. The good-hearted soul who goes around pouring out her philanthropy without first studying the situations to see what justice demands proves more upsetting than uplifting.

Suppose that your neighbor owed you a thousand dollars, and you in the goodness of your heart said: "I'll forgive that debt; forget it." And suppose you owed another neighbor a thousand dollars, and you go to him and say: "I've just forgiven a man his debt to me. Will you not therefore cancel my loan?" And suppose such generosity spread from person to person, would that guarantee a stable and equitable society? No, such mercifulness of spirit, divorced from a sense of divine justice, would be demoralizing. Mercy and forgiveness cannot be mere unregulated human emotions. They are jewels of the spirit, but they have value only in a setting of justice.

When we see that mercy is compassion based on justice, we must then go on to ask, what is it to be just? According to the Aristotelian principle, "Justice is a virtue of the soul distributing that which each person deserves." And when we come to decide what each person deserves, infinite understanding is required. Two prisoners stand before the same bar, charged with identical crimes. One grew up in the gashouse district of a city slum, with the street for his playground, and perhaps with a taint of weakness in his blood. The other had the advantages of a good home, splendid schools, and economic plenty. If the judge is to be just to those two prisoners, he must take account of all the mixed factors which entered into their lives. Or two boys sit in the same class at school. One is the placid type that takes things easily as they come; the other is tense, tying himself up in knots and tangling the threads of situations by his feverish intensity to find out the why of things. Unjust would it be to measure the ability and deportment of those two lads by the same yardstick of required courses and conventional behavior.

To render justice requires insight and imagination. Aye, does it not even call for a modicum of love? Can we do justice to the painter's canvas if we have no love for art? How then can we do justice to our fellow man, God's handiwork, if our hearts have not love? Mercy is compassion which involves justice, and that further involves imaginative understanding. Then we enter into that mystery of love where mercy and justice dwell together.

Furthermore, to be merciful toward another implies that the other is to some extent in our power, and that we can exact vengeance if we so desire. The crowd in the courtroom may pity the convicted prisoner, but it has no power in the matter of his punishment. The court, on the other hand, can show mercy by granting pardon or by imposing a lightened sentence. Thus mercy involves forbearance. And to hold back the hand in forbearance from one who has wronged us is far harder than to hold out the hand in sympathy or generosity to a stranger. Now begins to appear the barrier which makes mercy so difficult a virtue.

Before proceeding to the hurdle, perhaps we should pause to sum up our definition of mercy. It is active compassion based on justice, guided by understanding, illumined by love, and restrained by forbearance. The blind girl had the essence of its meaning when she said that mercy is the odor which flowers give when trampled upon.

WHY IS IT SO HARD TO BE MERCIFUL?

When we set out "to do justly and to love mercy," we so soon come up against the question of forgiveness. In a British broadcast just before the close of World War II, C. S. Lewis of Oxford declared: "Every one says forgiveness is a lovely idea, until they have something to forgive, as we have in war time. And then to mention the subject at all is to be greeted with howls of anger. . . . 'That sort of talk makes them sick,' they say. And half of you already want to ask me, 'I wonder how you'd feel about forgiving the Gestapo if you were a Pole or a Jew?' So do I. I wonder very much. . . . I am not trying to tell you in these talks what I could do. I can do precious little. I am telling you what Christianity is. I didn't invent it. And there, right in the middle of it, I find, 'Forgive us our sins, as we forgive those who sin against us.' There is no slightest suggestion that we are offered forgiveness on any other terms. It is made perfectly clear that if we don't forgive, we shall not be forgiven."

The difficulty of forgiving is deepened, the more we study what it involves. First of all, of course, it means to forego all private revenge, to remit the right to retaliate. Forgiving is somewhat different from excusing. We excuse a person's deed when we exempt him from the imputation of blame. For instance, we may say, "I excuse his conduct, considering the extraordinary provocation under which he acted." But I may forgive a person for behavior which I cannot excuse, because I still believe it blameworthy. Nevertheless, so far as my relations with him are concerned, I shall not hold his action against him.

Also, to forgive is not the same as to pardon. Pardon can come only from one who has the right to sit in judgment. A judge on the bench may pardon a prisoner for his crime; but though I am the one who has been wronged, I cannot pardon the fellow. Legally, only the authorized government can pardon a crime; morally, only God can pardon a sin. Nevertheless, I can forgive the man who hurts me, even though I cannot pardon him. Forgiveness is a change of attitude within the one wronged.

If, however, I am to forgive in the spirit of Jesus' teaching, I must go on to pray for God to pardon. I may abhor the wrong, being unable to excuse it or to pardon it; but if I call myself a follower of Christ, I go on praying for the soul of the wrongdoer.

We may refuse to seek revenge for an offence committed against us, and yet cherish such a lingering resentment against the offender that if he hurt himself, or if he lost his money, or if he made a fool of himself, or if his children turned out badly —well, we just would not be too sorry. In fact we might even find a secret and unholy satisfaction, such as Heine revealed when he wrote, only half in jest: "My wishes are a humble dwelling with a thatched roof, a good bed, good food, flowers at my window and some fine tall trees before my door. And if the Good God wants to make me completely happy, he will grant me the joy of seeing six or seven of my enemies hanging from the trees."

Christian forgiveness calls for a magnanimity which over-comes vindictiveness. The man of little soul does not rise above an injury. He remembers insults and allows grudges to fester. This streak of vindictiveness looks all the uglier when it runs through natures of large mental caliber. Michelangelo was a titan in talent, but when the ruling Pope's Master of Ceremonies criticized one of the artist's figures as more fit for a house of debauchery than for a place of worship, Michelangelo painted a portrait of his critic and put it in his picture of hell, and there left him to be the laughingstock of Rome.

Perhaps it is still more difficult to overcome jealousy than vindictiveness. One may have the grace to get along with those who are weaker than himself. Toward them he may be sympathetic, merciful, and helpful. And he may have the grace to get along with those who are stronger than he is. He may yield to their better judgment, and follow them faithfully and agreeably. But to get along with one's equals, to run side by side, compete for the same prizes, and yet to keep free from jealousy, that is almost the supreme test of a big nature.

Jealousy is a sin that gets into the little cracks rather than the large chasms. The office boy is never jealous of the company's president. But how frequently does the poison of jealousy seep into the little rivalries of the same profession, the same social circle.

Mercy faces its hardest task in overcoming the sin of being small. Smallness of nature is a sin so subtle that it does not disturb us much at the time. When a body stops growing, there is no pain such as attends a broken limb. When a mind stops growing, there is no ache. When a conscience ceases to grow, it suffers no twinge. The hardening of the heart, like the hardening of the arteries, may progress painlessly, until the damage is revealed by a paralyzing stroke. If sin means "missing the mark," as the Greek word implies, then failure to grow is sin. And because of their subtlety, Jesus spent more time on the sins of the cold heart than on those of the hot heart.

Christian forgiveness involves not only remitting the right to retaliate, and the removing of resentful feelings, even those of vindictiveness and jealousy, but also the effort to revive friendly relations. If we are to forgive, as Christ would have us, we must not stop with just calling it quits. Sometimes our attitude is something like this: "Yes, I forgive him, but I hope never to see him again." That is not good enough. Christ would have us go on and try to correct the wrongdoer. And in our effort at correction, we should make it clear to ourselves and to him that our motive is sincere good will. We should be sure to aim at helping him and not at humiliating him.

From ancient Greece comes the story, that Aristippus went on one occasion to his enemy Aeschines and said, "Shall we never be reconciled until we become table talk to all the country?"

Aeschines answered that he would most gladly be at peace.

Then Aristippus said: "Though I were the elder and better man, yet I sought first with thee."

Magnanimously Aeschines replied: "Thou art indeed a far better man than I, for I began the quarrel and thou the reconcilement."

To be sure, Aristippus had begun the process of forgiveness by going first to his enemy. So far, so good. But he almost spoiled the reconciliation by reminding Aeschines of his virtuous "firstness" in the gesture of forgiveness. It is not good enough to say, "I'll forgive but I can't forget"—that keeps resentment alive in my mind. And it is even worse to say, "I'll forgive but I won't let him forget"—that keeps resentment alive in both minds.

Yes, forgiveness and mercy are just about the loveliest notes in the harmony of living, but we spoil their appeal when we keep harping on them. Only love has the true touch, as Tennyson reminds us:

> Love took up the harp of life, and smote on all the
>   chords with might,
> Touched the chord of self, which trembling, passed in
>   music out of sight.

Such loving touch is granted only to those who graduate in the Master's school of forgiveness.

Who Can Be Merciful?

Since mercy involves forbearance and forgiveness, who is able to attain unto such godliness?

There is no gainsaying the gospel assertion that the mercy to be shown us depends on the mercy we show. Jesus made this unmistakably plain in his parable of the unmerciful servant who owed his royal master ten thousand talents. When he was called on to pay, he made an impassioned plea for mercy and was forgiven. Shortly thereafter, however, he accosted a fellow servant who owed him a trifling sum. Unable to collect, he cast the poor debtor into prison. When the news of this reached the king, he was wroth at his unmerciful servant and delivered him to the tormentors until he should pay all that was due. After finishing this parable, Jesus added: "So likewise shall my heavenly Father do also unto you, if ye from your hearts forgive not everyone his brother their trespasses."

Portia put the same truth cogently in her plea to Shylock:

> Consider this,
> That, in the course of justice, none of us
> Should see salvation: we do pray for mercy;
> And that same prayer doth teach us all to render
> The deeds of mercy.

And John Wesley used the same argument with Governor Oglethorpe of the Georgia colony. It happened that a servant had broken open and drunk several bottles of the governor's rare wine. Wesley interceded for the trembling offender, and tried to calm the enraged Oglethorpe. "Sir," shouted the irate governor, "I never forgive." "Then," calmly replied Wesley, "I hope you never offend."

Yet while we cannot get around the fact that our future pardon depends on our showing a forgiving spirit, we can hardly believe that our Lord was holding out a self-centered motive for being merciful. Jesus never bribed men to be good. Nor is he here hiring men to be merciful with offers of mercy. The Christian is to be merciful not because of the mercy he hopes to receive in the future, but because of the mercy he has received in the past.

The ability to be merciful arises not from the fear of future punishment, nor from the sidewalk view of our fellow men, who by their greed and selfishness make the idea of forgiveness at first seem silly and impossible. The gospels make it clear that we must look to God for the power to forgive before we look at the people to be forgiven. When Jesus commanded his disciples: "Love your enemies, bless them that curse you, do good to them that hate you," he added: "That ye may be the children of your Father which is in heaven; for he maketh his sun to rise on the evil and on the good, and sendeth rain on the just and on the unjust." It is the magnanimous quality of God's fatherhood rather than the surface appearance of man's brotherhood which begets the forgiving and merciful spirit.

On the wall of a downtown business office hangs the picture of the executive's father, a rugged but benign type of man with integrity and benevolence reflected in his features. One can well imagine how often that face of the father has steadied and restrained and strengthened the son amid the frictions and factions of the city's competitive life.

We look up from the crowd immersed in its selfish struggle of getting even and taking mean advantages and we behold our heavenly Father, who magnanimously sends his sunshine on the evil and on the good, who "so loved the world, that he gave his only begotten Son, that whosoever believeth on him should not perish but have everlasting life." And then we watch that Son, living, loving, and at last dying for his fellow men. As he hangs on the cross, we hear him pray with his parting breath for his crucifiers: "Father, forgive them, for they know not what they do." The sight of the people around so often makes us think of the bad things done *to* us; the vision of God and his suffering Son turns our thoughts to the good things done *for* us. And our hearts begin to mellow.

That the degree of our "forgivingness" depends on the depth of our sense of indebtedness was shown that day when Jesus was dining at the house of Simon the Pharisee. While he was at table, a woman of the street came in, bearing a precious bottle of perfume, which she broke, and then proceeded to anoint the Master's feet. Simon, the very proper and pious host, was shocked, and assumed that Jesus would see what type of woman she was and send her away. Jesus, divining Simon's thoughts, told a parable of a certain money lender, who forgave two of his debtors, one for five hundred shillings and one for fifty. Then Jesus asked his host, "Which of them therefore will love him the most?" Simon answered and said, "He, I suppose to whom he forgave the most." Jesus replied, "Thou hast rightly judged." Then he added, pointing to the woman: "Her sins, which are many, are forgiven, for she loved much; but to whom little is forgiven, the same loveth little."

When, like Simon the Pharisee, we look around and think ourselves about as good as the average and hence not much in need of forgiveness, our springs of mercy dry up. But if, like that penitent woman, we feel overwhelmingly indebted to God in Christ for his mercy toward us, our hearts are mellowed, and we pour out our gratitude and mercy in uncalculating measure.

And when we start with the thought of God's forgiving love, we begin to get an understanding of those human frailties which make men forgivable. We see what Browning's Rabbi Ben Ezra had in mind when he talked about "instincts immature" and "purposes unsure," and those factors in our

human makeup which "the low world from level stand" fails
to appraise.

The French have a saying, "He who understands all,
forgives all." The kernel of truth in that proverb is very
large. It can, of course, be made too soft. But when we try to
look with God's compassionate understanding, we withhold
our hasty judgments. Jesus said, "Judge not, that ye be not
judged." Certainly he could not have meant that we are not
to form judgments about the conduct of others. Jesus judged
sometimes tenderly, as in the case of the woman taken in
adultery, sometimes severely in hot language, as in the case of
the "whited sepulchres." So must we judge.

But the context of Jesus' words about judging serve to clarify his meaning. We are not to judge except as we are willing
to be judged. We are to be more severe in appraising ourselves
than in judging others. We are to treat our fault as a beam
to be removed, a big task, before we try to remove the mote
from our brother's eye, a comparatively small and delicate
operation.

Harold Bosley states: "A true judgment of another is one
kept humble by the realization of our kinship with one another, kept merciful by the realization that we too have sinned,
. . . kept responsible by the realization that we too have an
infinite obligation to help an erring one towards the path of
righteousness."

When we look at an enemy in the spirit of Christ, we are
disposed to feel that it is the evil in him, and not the man himself, which is hostile to us. "He is not himself." Hence, with
Augustine, our prayer should be against the malice of our enemy, that it may die and he may live.

In Hawthorne's *Transfiguration*, the very human Miriam
says to the puritanical Hilda: "You have no sin nor any con-

ception of it; therefore you are so terribly severe; as an angel you are not amiss, but as a human creature you need a sin to soften you."

Angels might prove rather difficult for us human creatures to live with. That is not an immediate problem for most of us, because not many of us are housed with perfect angels! But the persons we lovingly call "angelic" are not severe and unforgiving. They are not merciless toward temptations they do not feel. They do not need sin to soften them, as Hawthorne's Miriam suggested, but they have a sympathetic understanding of sinners. They have caught the spirit of him of whom it is written: "We have not an high priest which cannot be touched with the feeling of our infirmities; but was in all points tempted like as we are, yet without sin."

When we truly comprehend the compassionate nature of Christ, the high priest, we respond to the injunction: "Let us, therefore, come boldly to the throne of grace that we may obtain mercy and find grace to help in time of need." We see God ruling from a throne of justice, but we also see a "rainbow round the throne." Divine Justice wears as its halo the symbol of mercy. That makes it a "throne of grace."

And the stairs by which we can climb boldly to that throne where mercy is dispensed and mercifulness is caught begin to loom out of the shadow of seeming impossibility.

The pondering of God's mercies makes us feel humbly grateful and hopelessly in debt. We become "poor in spirit," as in the first Beatitude.

In the light of divine mercy we feel repentant for our failures and sins, and we feel responsible in part for the sins and sorrows of others. We join the company of those that mourn —as in the second Beatitude.

And then as we take the sufferings and shortcomings of

others to heart, we realize that all these cannot be remedied by our own cleverness, and that we must submit to God's training and tempering, that is we become meek—as in the third Beatitude.

And after we yoke ourselves to the Christ, who called himself meek and lowly of heart, and begin to share his passion for righting the world's wrongs, we find the hunger and thirst for righteousness growing within us—as in the fourth Beatitude.

Thus the first four Beatitudes appear as the steps by which we climb to the throne of grace where we "obtain mercy and find grace to help" in mercifulness. Mercy is no simple little "art of being kind." It is a high and holy virtue toward which we can climb only with divine help.

What Happens to the Merciful?

The quality of mercy is not strained;
It droppeth as the gentle rain from heaven
Upon the place beneath: it is twice blessed;
It blesseth him that gives, and him that takes.

When Portia's poetry is put into the prose of everyday living, how practical does it prove? The gentle rain seems a weak thing. But watch it falling on a plot of hard, dry, trampled earth. After awhile there is a softening, and life begins to push up through the mellowed ground. So with the mind of man. When we let the thoughts of divine mercies drop repeatedly on the gardens of our imaginations, our hearts are softened, as we have been saying. Then suppose we relax the tension of our set teeth through which we have been muttering, "I'll not be the first to forgive." And suppose we do take the first step toward reconciliation—well, have you ever tried it? If you have ever reached out your hand to one who has wronged you, then you know how the icicled springs of the heart are thawed. When goodness is returned for evil, the result is said to be the heaping of coals of fire on the head of the wrongdoer. Such heat causes him to burn with shame, but the better and more important effect is to melt the heart. What tears so refreshing as the tears of reconciliation between estranged friends, between a wife and a wayward husband, between a parent and a prodigal son. Truly, mercy blesses the giver as the gentle rain from heaven blesses the hardened earth.

Also we can say that the person who shows mercy and forgiveness purges himself of the poison produced by hatred and resentment. He gets a peace of mind and health of spirit not enjoyed by the unforgiving. The Nazi party in Germany, seeking a slogan for their rise to power, found one in "Death to the Jews." They held that hatred in their minds until some six million Jews were liquidated. But in doing so, they poisoned their own minds and developed unspeakable cruelties which were the product of their perverted thinking.

In contrast with such self-poisoning through the unforgiving attitude, think of the cleansing and calm which come through forgiveness. Sir Thomas More, Lord Chancellor of England, having been condemned to death in a high-handed court on specious grounds, addressed his judges thus: "More have I not to say, my Lords, but that Saint Paul held the clothes of those who stoned Stephen to death, and as they are now both saints in heaven, and shall continue there friends forever; so I verily trust, and shall most heartily pray, that though your lordships have now here on earth been judges to my condemnation, we may nevertheless hereafter cheerfully meet in heaven in everlasting salvation." When a man can say that to men who have just condemned him to death, he is showing a peace and magnanimity of mind which are the divine fruits of the forgiving spirit.

And mercy is twice blessed, for its blessings show in him that takes as well as in him that gives. Compassion has creative power. There was that poor woman of the street about to be stoned for her sin. When she was brought before Jesus, he did not add to her embarrassment by looking at her. He stooped and wrote in the sand, giving her time to pull herself together. Then he turned to the crowd, saying, "Let him that is without sin cast the first stone." No stones fell. Then turning to her, he said, "Doth no man condemn thee? Neither do I. Go and sin no more." In that woman's heart the smoking flax he did not quench. It flared up into a pure flame.

Again and again our Lord cupped with his compassion the flickering flame of faith and hope until it was restored. How tragic when the smoking flax is quenched!

This creative compassion is revealed in every sphere of life. Yonder is a child "crying its heart out." Its tears may be for some trifling thing, as we think, a broken toy, a lost pet. But what if nobody ever took that child up, wiped away its tears, and nestled its little panting heart against some comforting bosom. It was said of Byron as an explanation of his perversities that he was poorly mothered. In children's wards over the beds is often to be seen the sign "L. T. C." Those letters look like the designation of some of the landing craft used in the war. But "L. T. C." in the hospital stands for the words, "Loving Tender Care." And truly such care is part of the landing craft by which babies are landed on the shore of life.

The might of mercy is beyond measure, for it eludes the yardstick of the market place. It binds individuals together in families. Families can not be kept united on the basis of cold, calculating justice. Who can measure the just wages of a mother? And if mercy is the cement which holds households together, why not families of nations? Does that mean soft appeasement of other nations' selfish policies? No, for mercy involves justice; but remember, it is justice illumined by imagination, deepened by sympathy and restrained by forebearance.

But with all the blessings which mercy imparts to the giver and receiver, does it beget mercy? Do the merciful obtain mercy from men as well as from God? Certainly the converse is true. Mercilessness begets mercilessness. The Romans were merciless toward their barbarian neighbors, and when the latter conquered Rome, they showed no mercy to the Romans. The Germans in World War I were merciless toward their enemies, and they received little mercy at Versailles. The Czar's government was heartless toward the Russian peasants, and when the Revolution of 1917 put the peasants in power, they showed no mercy toward their former oppressors. An American official in our embassy at Moscow said to us in the summer of 1946 that we must remember that the idea of charity has been practically removed from the Soviet government's thinking. They think only of what they call rights. They do not understand what we call charity. That fact may help to explain something of the present Russian attitude to America's European Relief Program. They cannot understand why we should be helping Europe in the spirit of charity. They mistakenly assume we are prompted only by imperialistic desire for power. The unchristian attitude of the old Czaristic autocracy perverted the idea of charity in that land, and the world is now reaping the results.

Yes, mercilessness breeds mercilessness. But does mercy beget mercy? Wendell Willkie said that he found in China reservoirs of good will. What caused those? It was the gentle rain of mercy falling from the Christian missionaries through a century and more of service. It was the flood of mercy which America poured back into China after the Boxer uprising. Retaliation was then in our power, but instead of revenge we used the indemnity for further service to China, thereby forming a reservior of good will which has kept fresh the friendship between China and the United States.

The spirit of mercy and forgiveness is bound, as a general rule, to beget a softened spirit in others. Jesus declared the law of reciprocity: "Forgive, and ye shall be forgiven. Give, and it shall be given unto; . . . for with the same measure that ye mete withal it shall be measured to you again."

> Be noble! and the nobleness that lies
> In other men, sleeping, but never dead,
> Will rise in majesty to meet thine own.

Such is the law and the gospel as given in the New Testament. To be sure we are always hearing about exceptions to this general rule. We are ever being reminded that there are persons and nations who will not respond to forgiveness and magnanimity. But the question for us is, are we to make ourselves bitter by looking ever at the seeming exceptions to God's law, or are we to make ourselves better by looking at God's law of forgiveness and obeying it?

Jesus' own career seems the abject denial of the promise that the merciful shall obtain mercy from their fellow men. The supreme demonstrator of mercifulness, he was denied mercy and put to death on the cross. Yet when we hear him praying for his crucifiers, we witness the defeat of mercilessness; and we are haunted by the might of his mercy, which lures us and lifts us toward mercifulness as no comfortable conclusion could have done.

Forgiveness on our part cannot result in reconciliation and receive mercy until the other party repents. But the question for us is whether we are going as far as Christ would have us go in trying to awaken repentance. How oft shall my brother sin against me and I forgive him? "Seventy times seven?" Does that seem an infinity of forgiveness too great for our finite strength? Well, when we do our best and still keep trying, we touch "one able to do exceeding abundantly above all that we ask or think, according to the power that worketh in us."

Thus the law of forgiveness merges into the gospel of mercy.

VI. The Heart Has Eyes

Blessed are the pure in heart:
for they shall see God.

A MONG OUR five physical senses, the most dominant is the sense of sight. This fact was demonstrated by an intelligence test in a certain English school. A class of boys was sent into a room for two minutes and then brought back to write out a list of things noted while there. The lists jotted down by the lads varied in length from ten to forty objects. But the most significant aspect of those lists was that nothing was noted by the boys except the things which revealed themselves to the eye. In that room were the noises which came in from the street, the sound of a piano in another part of the building, the scent of a cigar purposely introduced; and yet not one of these was mentioned by the students.

HAVING EYES, SEE YE NOT?

Nevertheless, despite the potency and primacy of sight, our Lord once said, rebukingly, "Having eyes, see ye not?"

Recall the occasion. Jesus had fed the multitudes. Great crowds had been following him out of curiosity. Impressed by his power to heal and feed, the Pharisees asked for a sign, some spectacular evidence of his Messiahship. To get away from these sightseers and sign-seekers, he took ship with his disciples and sailed across the lake.

Then he turned to his own little company and he said, "Beware of the leaven of the Pharisees." The disciples looked bewildered, thinking he was talking about their bread. Jesus, seeing that even his own disciples did not understand him, said, "Having eyes, see ye not?"

As that question comes sighing across the centuries, does it strike any of us? Speaking very personally, I confess that it wakes me up. I realize how little I am seeing in comparison with what some around me find.

For instance, I think of the musician, born blind, who described his world as one of sound and melody. A friend procured for him a copy in Braille of Keats's "Ode to the Nightingale." As the blind man absorbed through his finger tips the lines of that poem, he exclaimed, "When Keats wrote that, he was living in my world." And I wonder how much I miss in the world of Keats and that sightless musician.

Or when I hear Sir James Jeans speak of astronomical phenomena as "messages in cipher" which we must learn to decode "out of their space-time wrappings," I feel about as ignorant as when I stand in a telegraph office watching the face of the operator while he decodes the flashes which are meaningless to me.

Or I think of the wealth of beauty seen by the artists. Perhaps I possess an average man's appreciation of nature, but I very much fear I should deserve the rebuke once given by the artist Turner to a sightseer who stopped to watch him at work. Looking over the artist's shoulder, this superficial critic said, "Why, Mr. Turner, I never saw any such light and color in nature as you put in your canvas." Turner merely replied: "Don't you wish you could? As for me, I never can hope to match with pigments the glory I see in the sky."

Or consider what mystic insights into reality some saintly souls get. A friend some few years ago was traveling in Switzerland with Stanley Jones, the devout and distinguished missionary to India. At a turn in their path, a majestic mountain peak loomed into breath-taking view. At sight of it Stanley Jones broke forth into conversation with God just as naturally as if the divine Presence were there in the form of a third companion. In that moment he saw the Lord as the prophet Isaiah saw him in the temple centuries ago. Yet that is a sight which many of us have missed in our tours of Switzerland.

Yes, around us are musicians who revel in richer worlds of melody, scientists who range wider reaches of knowledge, artists who catch deeper insights of beauty, saintly mystics who find more revelations of divinity—all of which make me feel that Jesus was speaking to me when he said, "Having eyes, see ye not?" And when we think of how much the Master saw in life, of how much he made out of the meager materials which barren Palestine afforded and how little we make out of this lush, rich America, we are aroused to ask why we are missing so much.

The reason is that we have three organs of vision, and our obsession with the first causes us to neglect the potentialities of the other two.

Suppose you were to go to your oculist tomorrow to be fitted with glasses. He would put you before a wall chart on which there were lines of letters, varying in size. He would fit a spectacle frame on your nose, and drop in lenses of differing strength. After a while he gets to what he thinks is about the right vision. And he asks about certain letters, "Can you see those?" And you say, "I see." That is physical vision.

Or tomorrow you go to consult a lawyer about your income tax. He explains the income tax laws, perhaps as much as income laws can be explained! The light of understanding begins to break on your mind and you say, "I see." That is mental vision.

But now suppose a daughter comes home to dinner tomorrow night. She goes through the meal with what she thinks is her usual composure. She believes she has herself under perfect control and is revealing none of her inner feelings. Across the table sits her mother. The mother detects a suppressed emotion in her daughter. After a while the mother says: "Mary, out with it; I see there's something up." That mother is seeing with the eyes of the heart.

THE EYES OF THE MIND

We all know that the state of the mind affects our seeing. A father and son walk down the road. The father is interested in nature. He sees the different kinds of grasses, trees, and flowers. The boy is interested in motor cars. He keeps track of how many Pontiacs and Plymouths pass. What a person has in mind conditions what he takes into his mind.

At the time Jesus said to his disciples, "Beware of the leaven of the Pharisees," he saw what was happening to them. They were catching the spirit of the Pharisees and the sightseers, who were motivated by curiosity. They were getting into the groove of the crowd thinking. To get them out of this groove, he took them across the lake. We all have a tendency to gravitate toward the viewpoint of those around us, our social set, our professional group. We see issues from the side our crowd is on. We choose the magazines, the books, even the preachers who give us what we want to hear. And these agents and agencies in their desire to please often become followers rather than leaders of public opinion. The journalism that is afraid not to conform to popular taste is "yellow." And there are yellow pulpits too! It was against this all too common tendency that Paul warned, saying, "Be not conformed to this world: but be ye transformed by the renewing of your minds that ye may prove what is that good and acceptable and perfect will of God."

Christ would have his followers get away from the crowd at times in order to clarify their vision. Jesus often went alone to pray. We must change our sights in order to get fresh insights. That is the one reason for religious worship. At worship we focus our minds on the things that are invisible and eternal; then when we turn back to the things that are seen and temporal, we see them with new and clearer insight.

When we look at our world with the eyes of the mind freshened by divine insights as Christ would have us, we see things with a positive rather than a negative outlook. Consider any local community. One man lives in that town with a negative, critical attitude. He sees the pettiness of its people, the stodginess of the place, all the tawdry things that Sinclair Lewis portrayed in *Main Street*. Another man lives in the town, and sees the heartiness of its neighborly spirit, the opportunities offered by its schools and churches, all the inviting things that a William Allen White would see in his community. It is the same town; the difference is in the set of the mental focus and the depth of insight.

Two persons survey the current world situation. One with a negative mind sees everything heading for war and chaos —the breakdown of peace negotiations in Europe, the collapse of orderly government in China, the spread of regimentation and communism. The other with an affirmative set of mind sees the rising humanitarianism of the world, that while we are multiplying our powers of destruction we are also increasing our means and passion for saving life. He sees the United Nations as halted at some points by vetoes and tensions and yet advancing in matters of health and education and human rights, and already solving several situations which once would have provoked war. He sees the rising conscience of the world making protest against vicious trials of clerical leaders and remembers that not so long ago it was the custom to persecute men for their religious faith.

The follower of Christ tries to view the world with the affirmative mind of Christ. Jesus saw the world with the realism of a physician and the sensitivity of a Saviour. But as the Bible says, "In him was yea." He had a positive, affirmative outlook which saw the great verities of life as advancing. He knew his earthly career was nearing its Cross. Nevertheless he said, "My father worketh hitherto and I work"; and also "Greater works than these shall ye do because I go unto the Father." Jesus was confident his work was going on. When he saw his time was short, he said to his disciples, "I have many things to say unto you, but ye cannot hear them now. Howbeit when he, the Spirit of Truth, is come, he will guide you into all truth." He felt truth was going on. On the night before his death, he said to his followers, "In my Father's house are many mansions . . . I go to prepare a place for you." Jesus saw life, truth, goodness going on.

And that is the Christian's view of history, which we can catch if we look with the eyes of the mind, as Christ would have us look. Arnold Toynbee, toward the end of his book *A Study of History*, comes to this conclusion: "The One remains, the many change and pass. And this is in truth the final result of our study of saviors. . . . And now as we stand and gaze with our eyes fixed upon the farther shore, a single figure rises from the flood and straightway fills the whole horizon. There is the Savior; and 'the pleasure of the Lord shall prosper in his hand; he shall see of the travail of his soul and be satisfied.'"

The world is in travail but it is the birth pangs from which something better is being born, provided we have the mental vision and the moral valor. It comes back to Thomas Carlyle's old question, "Wilt thou be a hero or a coward?" In the breast of each one of us is an incessant dialogue between the coward in us who is out for safety and the hero in us who is out for victory. Both view the same situations. But the coward would wait until he can see through beyond the shadow of a doubt, while the hero starts with the shadows of doubt thick upon him. And doing the duty next to him and the duty next to that, he eventually comes through. Such is the testimony of Christian experience.

With the eyes of our minds, if we lift up our downcast gaze, we can see the things that are invisible and invincible and eternal.

THE EYES OF THE HEART

The other reason why we are missing what Jesus saw is that we are not looking with the eyes of the heart.

When we think of the heart as the seat of the emotions, we know how much its state affects what we see, even with our physical eyes. A doctor told recently of a husband and wife who drove from New York to the Middle West. The wife did the driving, for she was an excellent chauffeur. Out in the west, the husband was stricken and died. The grief so affected the wife's vision that she could not drive again for weeks.

And our heart feelings affect our mental vision far more than our physical vision. When Paul writes to the Ephesians, he prays: "May God grant you the spirit of wisdom and revelation for the knowledge of himself, illuminating the eyes of your heart." If we are to see God and God's children as Christ would have us see them, we must use the eyes of the heart.

Watch the crowd as it observes the news of the world on the screen. Does the mere sight of people of other nations evoke friendly response from our fellow sitters? Not often. Mere sight does not breed friendship. Cold facts seem to be producing cold wars. Our information about other races and nations must be illumined with Christlike imagination. We must catch the human feelings behind the cold statistics of the starving and the homeless. We must try to enter into the emotions of those little children of China as they hunt for food among the garbage. We must try to put ourselves in the dock with men who are brought to court on false charges and denied fair trial.

Imagination is even more needed than information in begetting brotherhood among the peoples of the earth. At this point religion has an imperatively important part to play. If a curtain be drawn across a room, those on one side cannot see those on the other. But if there be a mirror in the ceiling of the room, those on both sides of the curtain can look up into the mirror and thereby look down into the places of the others. So in our world now divided by curtains, both "iron" and paper, those who sincerely look up in prayer to God, the Father of all men, are enabled to see with the eyes of the heart behind the curtains. This practice, repeated often enough, progressively sensitizes the imagination toward an understanding of those whose color and creeds and culture are different.

And the eyes of the heart are essential when we look toward God. "The natural man seeth not the things of God; they are spiritually discerned." A very thoughtful woman asked recently, "How can we know when we are doing the will of God?" It recalled the medieval saint who in the agony of prayer cried, "O that I certainly knew!" Then he seemed to hear a voice saying: "What wouldst thou do if this certain knowledge were bestowed on thee? Do now what thou wouldst then, and rest secure."

Such is the attitude in which we are to seek assurance of God's will. "Blessed are the pure in heart," said Jesus, "for they shall see God." He knew that we give up prayer or find it unreal usually not because of intellectual difficulties but because of something we will not forgive, some envy that discolors our vision, some film of fear or dull neglect which clouds our spirits.

The Pure in Heart—Who?

But what is it to be pure in heart? James Moffatt once said in class that this Beatitude should be translated thus: "Blessed are they who are not double-minded, for they shall be admitted into the intimate presence of God." The Epistle of James indicates a similar meaning when it says: "Purify your hearts, ye double-minded."

The expression, "double-minded" suggests instability, unsettledness, perhaps even deceitfulness. A person may be double-minded because he lacks integration. He thinks one way today and another way tomorrow, or he is moved one way by one side of his nature and a different way by the other side of his nature. Or a person may be double-minded because he lacks integrity. He thinks one way and speaks another. He has two reasons for what he does—a good reason which he announces and a real reason which he keeps to himself. But whether the double-minded man merely lacks integration or whether he lacks integrity, he is unstable. We cannot be quite sure of him because he is not sure of himself. And if we wish to make sure of God, we must first try to make ourselves the kind of persons of whom God and our fellow men can be sure.

The pure in heart are those who are not double-minded,

unstable, deceiving themselves and others. They are single-minded and wholehearted.

The first step toward such purity of heart is to have a will single to the good. Kierkegaard declared that purity of heart is to will only one thing and that the Good. In starting with the will, Kierkegaard is in line with our Lord. When his listeners were discussing his authority, Jesus laid down this test: "If any man will to do his [God's] will, he shall know of the doctrine whether it be of God or whether I speak of myself." The Master was trying to make clear that doing right is a requisite to correct thinking.

Conduct conditions thinking as thinking conditions conduct. Among the ancient Corinthians was a saying, "Eat and drink, for tomorrow we die." We might say that their sensual living was the result of their lack of belief in immortality. Or we might say that it was their sensual indulgence which dimmed their faith in an immortal future. Both statements would be true; but when we survey the New Testament as a whole, it would seem that conduct shapes belief even more than belief shapes conduct. Note the frequent use of the word, "walk." "Walk in love," "walk in the light," "walk in newness of life." We enter into truth feet first even more than head first. The things we miss seeing are the things we miss being.

As Browning's Bishop Blougram put it to the skeptic: "Like you this Christianity or not? Has it your vote to be so if it can?" But remember this means willing the good because it is the good and not because we shall get some reward from it. That is a pretty searching test when we put it to ourselves.

And to have a will single to the good means that we desire it for itself and not because we wish to escape punishment for the bad. In fact, if we really wish the good, we shall welcome the punishment as medicine to make us well and good. A carpenter in California killed his wife in a burst of passion. He was sentenced to life imprisonment. Because his act was unpremeditated and his prison record was excellent, his lawyer later applied for a reduction of sentence. The prisoner refused to make the plea because he said he wanted to take the punishment and thus "show Mary that I am sorry and still love her."

If we would be pure in heart, we must begin by having a will single to the good because it is the good, and for no other reason.

The second step is to have an eye single to the good and the true. Jesus put emphasis on that. He said, "If thine eye be single, thy whole body shall be full of light." If we have one eye out for the good and the other eye out for the evil, or one eye looking for God and the other eye looking out for our self-interest, we darken our minds. That was the trouble, for example, with Pilate. When Jesus was brought to him charged with claiming to be king, Pilate asked, "Art thou a king?" Jesus answered, "To this end was I born, and for this cause came I into the world that I should bear witness unto the truth. Every one that is of the truth heareth my voice." Pilate then asked, "What is truth?" Jesus did not deign to reply. There was no use in trying to expound truth to Pilate for he did not have an eye single to its search. He had one eye out to help the prisoner because he felt him to be innocent, but he had his other eye out to please the people and Caesar.

If we want to know the truth, we must be of the truth, that is we must have an eye single to it. This principle applies to every realm. In this foggy world of ours, clouded by propaganda and politics, we say, "Oh, if I could only know the facts about Europe, or about Russia, or about China!" Well, there is one thing we can all do. We can ask ourselves if we are sufficiently free from prejudice and passion to follow the truth if we found it. Until we thus have an eye single to the good and the true, we shall not see the truth about men or God.

When we reach this stage, we are headed for the third requisite of the pure in heart, which is a mind single to the good, the true, and the beautiful, the ultimate values.

Single-mindedness is not narrow-mindedness or simple-mindedness, but a kind of genuineness, a soundness at the core, an indifference to externals. Ralph Adams Cram, the architect, was wont to say that a Christian church building should get better in structure and richer in materials, the farther in you go. Thus it becomes truly symbolic of Christian character.

When we set our will to do God's will and our eye to see God's purposes and our mind to think on whatsoever things are true, whatsoever things are honest, just, pure, lovely, and of good report, light begins to stream into our minds and to dispel the shadows of doubt; positive suggestions begin to drive out negative and weakening thoughts; good impulses begin to overcome evil—in short we cleanse the thoughts of our hearts by the inspiration of God's Holy Spirit. Thus we approach the state of the pure in heart.

They See God—How?

With will and eye and mind made single as described, we can turn our mental camera in almost any direction and get assuring pictures of God's presence. We can turn our gaze toward the heavens and say with the psalmist, "The heavens declare the glory of God, and the firmament showeth his handiwork." We can look at the earth and feel with Carlyle that Nature is the very garment of God. We can look at saintly souls in their goodness, at scientists in their search for truth, at poets with their flashes of beauty, and all these seem to reveal a God speaking through them.

But in order to test this vision of the pure in heart, let us, as they say in Hollywood, do one or two "retakes" of certain scenes in the divine drama where the record explicitly says the characters "saw God."

Look first at a young man back in Genesis. Jacob, when we first see him, is far from pure in heart. He cheats his brother Esau out of his birthright. He swindles Laban out of some property. Then he returns to the land of his father where he is to meet Esau again. The night before that meeting, Jacob is alone, his flocks and family having gone on ahead. There in the darkness Jacob wrestles through the night with an invisible antagonist. We may call that invisible wrestler the angel of God or Jacob's own better self. The record is that his character was changed. And Jacob, who now becomes Israel because he has power with God, cries, "I have seen God face to face and my life is preserved." Jacob's will and eye and mind had been set in focus on God, and then a moral struggle clicked the camera and he caught a vision of God. The revealing glimpse of God may come in some moral crisis which cracks the shell of pretense and tests the purity of heart.

Turn now from Jacob to Job. When we first see Job, everything is prospering with him. He serves God in order that God may reward him handsomely. Job's religion is of that "success psychology" type which is so popular with many people. God is the great giver of benefits, a sort of divine Santa Claus.

Such a self-centered, success-seeking attitude crumbled when Job suffered a succession of calamities. Finally a voice out of the whirlwind lifts Job's gaze upward to the greatness of a Creator who laid the foundations of the earth and made the morning stars sing together. And as Job's will and eye and mind become centered on God rather than on himself, the light breaks on Job's mind and he cries: "I have heard of thee by the hearing of the ear, but now mine eye seeth thee." Job's heart had become pure toward God.

Review the change wrought in another character. On the road from Jerusalem to Damascus, Saul surrendered his will to God as revealed to him in Christ, whom he had been persecuting. His name having been changed from Saul to Paul, he set his will and eye and mind so singly toward this Christ that he said to the Corinthians, "I determined not to know anything among you save Jesus Christ and him crucified." He so identified his life with Christ that he came to say, "For me to live is Christ." Then listen to him as he nears the end of the long road, having invested his time, his talents, his life in the service of this Master: "I know whom I have believed and I am persuaded that he is able to keep that which I have committed unto him against that day." No longer any uncertainty or guessing. Paul knew. Having given himself single-mindedly and whole heartedly to God in Christ, he was sure of God.

If these scriptural situations seem a bit too remote and spectacular, we may add the experience of Horace Bushnell. After laboring for years in his Hartford parish, he awoke one morning at the age of forty-six, crying, "I see it, I see it." Asked to explain, he said, "The Gospel. It is not the committing of one's thought in assent to any proposition, but the trusting of one's being, there to be rested, kept, guided, molded, governed, and possessed forever."

Bushnell was one of those who by faithfully practicing the presence of God, sometimes plodding along by sheer singleness of will, are at last admitted into the intimate presence of the Most High.

Professor G. A. Johnston Ross was ever stressing to his classes at Union Theological Seminary that the primary purpose of every sermon, as well as of the worship service, was to make men aware of God, for if they could feel the Divine Presence, most of their problems would assume a different aspect. "Seeing God" imparts a strength to find solutions and thus renders unnecessary so many specific pulpit prescriptions.

When Tennyson was advanced in years, he asked his son, who was to be the executor of his estate, to see that the publishers, when they collected his poems and put them into a single volume, should put "Crossing the Bar" at the end of the book. Why Tennyson made such a request we are not told. But we remember that when he was once asked what was his dearest wish, he answered, "A clearer vision of God." It would therefore seem an appropriate climax that the last lines in his volume of collected poems should read:

> And though from out this bourne of time and place
> The flood may bear me far,
> I hope to see my Pilot face to face
> When I have crossed the bar.

The pure in heart see their Pilot face to face.

VII. What the World Seems to Want Most

Blessed are the peacemakers:
for they shall be called the children of God.

SOME THIRTY months after the guns ceased firing in World War II, a radio questionnaire was submitted as to what the world wanted most from America. The conclusion drawn from the answers was that the primary desire was for peace. The volume of discussion in public press and private circles would seem clearly to support the radio poll.

When we say that we desire peace, what do we have in mind? In view of the tense world situations current, most of us think at once of peace between nations. When the air is filled with warnings and national budgets are pyramided skyward by the fear of future war, all thoughtful persons pray fervently for international peace. They see that global conflicts in the atomic age mean the suicide of civilization.

But if we should prove able to resolve the international tensions and to organize the family of nations under world law, would we then enjoy peace? Several lands have been recently reddened with blood although they were not at war with any other country. Peace between nations does not guarantee peace within nations.

And if we could organize our national economy to do away with industrial and racial conflicts, some of us would still remain at strife within our social and domestic circles. In fact, many persons are so taken up with frictions in their near-at-hand situations that they give little thought to large social and world problems. The soldier who wrote to his wife begging her to stop nagging him so that he could "fight this war in peace" was revealing a mood by no means isolated, which seeks escape from personal strife by engaging in large public conflicts.

But we might be domestically adjusted and economically secure, and yet still be full of inner tensions. Joshua Liebman began his best-selling book *Peace of Mind* with the statement that in his youth he had made a list of earthly desirables—health, love, riches, beauty, talent, power, fame, and a few others. Showing his list to a wise older friend, he was told that he had left out one ingredient without which every other possession becomes a hideous torment. That one thing is peace of mind.

Starting on his search for this essential attribute, peace of mind, Dr. Liebman produced a book which struck a responsive chord in the hearts of millions—a fact which was not only a tribute to the author's ability but also a revelation of the readers' interest. The craving for inner peace and contentment seems ever more visible and vocal.

WHERE PEACEMAKING BEGINS

"The longest journey begins with the first step." For the peacemaker, that first step is with himself.

If a person is not at peace within himself, he is pretty sure to be at odds with other people. The man whose own life is not orderly is like a ship whose ballast has become loose. And a ship with loosened ballast rolls unmanageably, a menace to itself and to other craft. He who feels frustrated easily becomes the tool of the agitator and the warmonger.

"If a house be divided against itself, that house cannot stand." That truth is so characteristic of Jesus' teaching that it was caught by all the Synoptists. The Carpenter of Nazareth came to reconstruct divided houses into unified homes of the soul.

Sometimes a life is divided between its inner self and its outer selves. As William James said, a man has "as many different selves as there are distinct groups of persons about whose opinion he cares." And it may happen that in keeping up these external social fronts, he develops a strain of pretense which is fatal to his peace of mind. When a person is using his energy to conceal an inner emptiness behind a pretentious façade, when he is struggling to maintain a reputation at variance with his true character, such a man is a house divided against itself.

Jesus would have us be concerned about the front we put up toward other people. Even as we should not erect a house which is an eyesore to the public, so we should not present a personality which is unattractive, surly, and unpleasant. Such externals affect our neighbors' peace of mind. Nevertheless, we are to seek peace within ourselves by first becoming sound at the center.

> To thine own self be true,
> And it must follow as the night the day
> Thou canst not then be false to any man.

But what if Polonius had given that sound advice to Hamlet rather than to Laertes? Would the distraught young Hamlet have understood what being true to himself involved? When a man is beside himself with anger or distress, he cannot identify his true self to which he is to be true. The Son of man renders a double service to the sons of men. He bids them be true to themselves, and he also shows them what their true selves are. He brings peace to the inner self by breaking the strain of pretense.

A second type of "house divided against itself" is the life which is torn between its forward drive and its backward pull. Physically we are so made that we move better through space going forward. But in moving through time, it is just the reverse. We can see what is behind us but we cannot see what will happen tomorrow. And because we have to move through both time and space, we human beings often develop tensions between our forward and backward tendencies.

Jesus was very familiar with lives thus divided. "No man having put his hand to the plough, and looking back, is fit for the Kingdom of God." When a person continues to look back to something he should put behind him, when he keeps reopening yesterday's decisions and weakening himself with futile regrets, he is not fit to be a peacemaker, for he has not found the secret of peace.

To correct this forward-backward tension, Jesus taught us to cut ourselves loose from part of the past. "Let the dead bury their dead." Such was the Master's short surgical way of saying that we are simply to turn our backs on some things and go ahead. When a decision is made or a contract is signed, do not keep the rear gate of the mind open so that yesterday's pack of hounding worries will rush in to spoil today's peace of mind.

But Jesus does more than merely bid us turn our backs on what is behind us. When the mind of Christ becomes "the master light of all our seeing," the region of recollection is so transformed that good memories remain and the evil ones are blotted out. He turns us from remorse, which is futile regret for a past that cannot be changed, to repentance, which is a redemptive turning toward the future. As Maeterlinck says:

"In owning our faults we disown them; and in confessing our sins, they cease to be ours." Christ "breaks the power of cancelled sin," "sets the prisoner free"—free from the lure of the old temptation, free from the bondage of habit.

But most destructive to our inner peace is the division between our higher and lower natures. We are "such stuff as dreams are made on"; we are also such stuff as animals are made of. Who does not understand Paul's self-analysis: "The good that I would I do not; but the evil which I would not, that I do. . . . I delight in the law of God after the inward man; but I see another law in my members, warring against the law of my mind, and bringing me into captivity to the law of sin which is in my members."

Sometimes we think we can get rid of this inner conflict by letting down and living on the lower animal level, "doing what comes naturally." The Prodigal Son tried that, but the husks of indulgence did not satisfy him indefinitely. Augustine as a young man sought to find peace by every form of sensual pleasure, but he discovered eventually that the soul is restless until it finds rest in God. Francis Thompson, the English medical student, tried to escape from his conscience by fleeing "down the nights and down the days," but he ever heard the "Hound of Heaven" breathing over his shoulder, "All things betray thee who betrayest me."

Christ comes to the man who is trying to find peace on the lower level of his nature, and he disturbs him "with the joy of elevated thoughts"; he sets him thinking on whatsoever things are true, honest, just, pure, lovely, and of good report; he creates an atmosphere of wholesomeness in which temptations tend to lose their power.

When Bishop Herbert Welch reached his eightieth birthday with such serenity of spirit and zest of living that he was the marvel of a large company gathered to honor him, he said: "As I get older, life becomes simpler because I see the essentials more clearly in the evening light." He had learned from Christ what things should have priority, what are ends and what are means. He had developed that singleness of eye which delivers from distracting side-views and that singleness of purpose which delivers from diverting side-issues. Is it accidental that the Beatitude of the peacemakers follows directly the blessing on the pure in heart? "The wisdom that is from above is first pure, then peaceable."

When the war clouds begin to appear on the horizon, the cry is soon heard in the streets that there is something which comes before peace, and that something is liberty. "It is better to die on one's feet than to live on one's knees." Of course we should prize liberty. And certainly we should not grovel on our knees before tyrants and dictators abroad or at home. But according to the Bible there is something that comes before both liberty and peace. And that something is righteousness. "And the fruit of righteousness is sown in peace of them that make peace." Righteousness is the soil from which peacemaking stems. And not so many of our fellow men would die on their feet as soldiers if more of us would get on our knees before God to seek his righteousness.

God, when given charge of an individual life, sets it in order as a mother straightens up a child's nursery when she puts away the toys which the little one has left littering the floor. So order was brought into Paul's life, enabling him to say: "I put away childish things; . . . now abideth faith, hope, love, these three; but the greatest of these is love." When a person has achieved such a peaceful ordering of his own life under the primacy of love, he is fit to be a peacemaker among others.

Roads to Reconciliation

The search for peace of mind may lead to softness and selfishness. We must not mistake peace-keeping for peace-making. We may keep the peace because we are too indifferent to care what goes on around us, or too good-natured to feel any righteous indignation at wrongdoing, or too selfish or lazy to risk any unpleasantness for the sake of setting things right.

Jesus could have kept this peace by remaining in the Galilean villages, basking in his popularity, healing the sick, preaching comfort. But he set his face toward Jerusalem where critics and a cross awaited him. His was a ministry of active reconciliation. "God was in Christ, reconciling the world unto himself." And God "hath given to us the ministry of reconciliation." The peacemaker is called, not to a sheltered, passive role, but to an active aggressive program.

By his very thoughts the peacemaker becomes a reconciling force. Having pure motives, he imputes worthy motives to others, giving the benefit of the doubt wherever possible. Living in the atmosphere of high ideals, he makes angry disputes seem mean in his presence. When trouble is brewing in any group, we usually know the persons to whom we can go to get the "low down," as we say. They are those who keep their ears down on the level where the "low down" is. And we also usually know the persons who can best bring the conflicting parties together. These are the peacemakers, who not only live on a higher level but lift others to it.

By his words as well as by his thoughts, the peacemaker is a reconciling influence. He speaks his convictions when a moral issue is at stake. He enters into controversies to correct falsehood, but "speaking the truth in love, he grows up into him in all things who is the head, even Christ." There are three levels of conversation. The highest is talk about ideas; the second highest is talk about things; the lowest is talk about persons. The peacemaker keeps above personalities in his controversies, even in his conversations, seeking the truth without disrespect to those who differ with him, counteracting prejudice, suspicion, and hatred by the sanity of his mind and the sympathy of his heart.

A prejudice is a judgment or opinion formed without due examination of the facts essential to a just and impartial determination. It is a learned response that has gotten into the subconscious and become fixed emotionally.

The forms of prejudice are manifold. That blind unreason which shutters the mind against the light of logic and refuses to look facts in the face—that is prejudice. Those little preconceptions which cause the mind to jump to conclusions without looking for reasons—this is prejudice. That cold predisposition which closes the heart against the approaches of affection and cruelly judges before it hears the defense—that is prejudice. That vampire of suspicion which flies about in the darkness of ignorance and sucks the blood of ruddy hopes and healthy enterprises—that is prejudice. That smouldering dislike of the different which can flame into a rage of hatred against foreigners and pioneers and saints and even saviors—that is prejudice.

Prejudice is a sin which every one denounces and almost no one seriously confesses. It is difficult to dislodge from the human mind because the possessor either does not think he has it or does not think it a dangerous sin if he has. Most of us admit that we have some prejudices and smile about them as if they were harmless foibles. Narrow-minded persons do not come crying to be saved from their prejudices. It is this self-deception and self-satisfaction which serve to make prejudice so baffling.

Whence come these prejudices of ours? It would seem at times that they derive from thin air. As was said by one of its victims, "Prejudice, like the spider, makes everywhere its home and lives where there seems nothing to live on." But when we look more closely we can discover some materials out of which these webs of prejudice are woven.

One of these sources is social inheritance. We are tattooed with the beliefs of our tribe while we are yet in our cradles. At a surprisingly early age we take on the unreasoned likes and dislikes of our families, our friends, our communities. If we would be peacemakers, we must watch the juncture between the older and younger generations in order to prevent the children from catching the prejudices of the parents. Also we should cultivate the viewpoint of the young in order to emancipate ourselves from our own narrow-mindedness. Jesus set a child in the midst of some Palestinian elders and said, "Except ye be converted and become as little children, ye shall not enter into the kingdom of Heaven."

A second source of prejudice is ignorance. We so often dislike because we do not know. In the apocryphal book The Wisdom of Solomon, the writer says: "They erred in the knowledge of God. . . . They lived in the great war of ignorance, and those so great plagues they called peace." The plagues which the world miscalled peace constituted the great war of ignorance—ignorance of God, ignorance of self, ignorance of others. The peacemaker seeks to learn and speak "the truth, the whole truth, and nothing but the truth." And though at his best, his mind wears the badge of its finitude, he is sufficiently free from fear and bias to follow the truth when he sees it.

In the early days of the Southern Confederacy, General Robert E. Lee was severely criticized by General Whiting. It might have been expected that Lee would wait for a time when he could get even with Whiting. A day came when President Jefferson Davis asked General Lee to come for consultation. Davis wanted to know what Lee thought of General Whiting. Without hesitation Lee commended Whiting in high terms and called him one of the ablest men in the Confederate army. An officer present motioned Lee aside to suggest that he must not know what unkind things Whiting had been saying about him. Lee answered: "I understood that the President desired to know my opinion of Whiting, not Whiting's opinion of me." There spoke the magnanimous spirit of the peacemaker, who pursues truth undeflected by personal interest.

By deeds as well as by thoughts and words, the peacemaker is a minister of reconciliation. He does not merely discuss the problems of brotherhood between racial and religious groups; he enters into the experiences of fellowship with individuals of other groups. He does not try to do by agitation what he fails to do by demonstration. He prepares for world citizenship by practicing the principles of brotherhood in his own community, for he knows that if he cannot get along with his neighbors it is futile to talk about a family of nations, and that if he does not keep his word as man to man, he is not consistent in asking governments to stand by their treaties.

The peacemaker takes seriously the command of the Lord: "Love your enemies, bless them that curse you, do good to them that hate you, and pray for them which despitefully use you and persecute you, that ye may be the children of your Father which is in heaven." A searching ethic indeed! But if we are to be called the children of God—and that is the explicit promise to the peacemakers—we must take it as our norm.

And the only hope of obeying such seemingly impossible commands is to live in the atmosphere of a loving heavenly Father. Horace Taft in his autobiography told how his birth discomfited his next older brother Willie—the future president, William Howard Taft. He wrote:

I did not know until nearly seventy years later that my welcome into this world was not unanimous. I was greatly tickled to run across a letter which I still possess, written on the day of my birth, December 28, 1861, by my father to my grandfather Torrey. After telling of the important arrival and of my mother's condition, he adds: "Willie is very much displeased about it and insists that old Santa Claus brought him here because no one else wanted him. Louise has, however, compromised the matter with him and the baby is to remain awhile, and if he does not behave well he is to be sent to the orphan asylum, but if he behaves well we may keep him. Harry is pleased with the new brother, but Willie wants no other brother than Harry." Evidently I behaved well, for I never went to the orphan asylum.

What changes the feeling of jealousy or rivalry which one child in a home might very naturally feel at the arrival of another child and the consequent division of attention and patrimony? It is the overarching parental love which encompasses the growing family. Likewise only the lively sense of God's fatherhood can beget the family feeling in our local and world communities.

Consider the degrees of love. In the child, the first form of love to appear seems to be a love of self, an instinctive desire to satisfy its bodily needs, to preserve and enlarge the self. Then comes love of parents, an outgoing, adoring affection for mother and father. A little later appears the love of friends, usually those of the child's own sex. After a while something in the youth's nature feeds that first pure flame of adolescent love, which shows in the radiant eyes of teen-age boys and girls. Later comes the love of mate, which forms the home and enriches the natures of both husband and wife. Normally this is followed by parental love, which is the highest form of natural affection, because the parent's devotion to a child persists even when it is not reciprocated.

Now all these forms of love are like the flame of the candle, in that they are fed by elements resident in our human nature which is lighted by them. But the incandescence of the electric light is caused by a current surging through the wires from a source beyond them.

Similarly with the love which Christ commanded us to have toward our neighbors, even our enemies, it must come from a source beyond our natural affections. We do not "fall in love" with the people on "the other side of the tracks" or on the other side of the equator. Good will toward them has to be generated. And Christ came to do that very thing.

He generates brotherly love and the reconciling spirit in ways too numerous to catalogue here. For one thing, he does it by ever charging our minds with the Gospel truth that God loves every individual regardless of how unattractive or unworthy such a one may look to us.

And to God each person is uniquely precious. Dean Ernest Melby declares that a schoolteacher should treat every child as if it were an irreplaceable object of art. There never was a duplicate of any child and there never will be. In a family if a child dies, other children may be born, but none can take the place of the little one that was lost. So our heavenly Father is a shepherd who leaves the ninety-and-nine to find the stray. Christ's is a Gospel of persons and not of percentages.

Jesus portrayed the appeal and poignancy of God's love in matchless parables. But word pictures cannot generate the divine love in passive spectators. Action is required if we are to lay hold on the power to love strangers, even enemies. Here are the directions: "If we walk in the light, as he is in the light, we have fellowship one with another." Not by mere talking, but by walking, do we catch the power to become peacemakers.

The road to reconciliation is to walk in the light as Christ is in the light.

The Fight for Fellowship

Human nature is made both for fighting and for fellowship. There is something in us that thrills to a fight and something in us that craves comradeship. This assertion is attested by the common sayings that men like a fighter and that all the world loves a lover. This normalcy and necessity of both fighting and fellowship are further evidenced by the fact that the one who so embodied the ideal of brotherhood that he has been called the Prince of Peace was the one who said, "I came not to send peace but a sword." The man of Nazareth was a fighter. But he was a fighter for fellowship.

Herein lies one major difference between the Master's attitude and our modern one. Jesus employed the fighting spirit to make for fellowship. We use it to destroy friendship. Jesus struck at the evil thing but strove to save the sinner. We, on the other hand, are prone to hate the sinner and then cherish the sin. Jesus hated the things that make for war, but he loved the enemy. We hate the enemy but cherish the things that make for war. Our fighting zeal is easily aroused against human foes, and not so quickly against inhuman systems. Thus the tragic trail of hatred has come down the centuries. We fight the warriors but keep the war system.

The paradox of peace is that we can have peace only by fighting for it. We must wage peace with the zeal and strategy that men have used in waging war.

To do that we must take certain great words on which war has had a monopoly and show that they belong to peace as well. One such word is patriotism. There are few nobler sentiments than love of country.

> Breathes there the man with soul so dead
> Who never to himself hath said
> This is my own, my native land?

But the trouble is that this patriotic emotion is seemingly stirred only by warlike things. It is in war time that we picture our country as a mother with a mailed fist at her throat. It is in war time that we listen to patriotic speeches which during peace we avoid as dull. It is to the men who fight in uniform that we ordinarily apply the word patriot. Our so-called patriotic societies nearly all have a military flavor and purpose. In short, the word patriotism has been monopolized by war.

Now, if we are to wage peace as men have waged war, we must stir patriotic sentiments by peaceful means as well as by warlike ones. Can this be done? Why not? Why can we not effect the same transformation in our love of country as in our love of persons? There was a time when men thought they had to arouse woman's love by fighting for it with physical prowess. The knight won his fair lady by defeating his rival in duelling combat. But today if it were known that two suitors engaged in a fight over a woman's hand, it is fairly certain that neither would get her. There was a time when public leaders won their following by physical prowess. Saul's strength helped to make him king in a primitive day. But if a leader in our government should stoop to settle his quarrels in bodily combat, the public would lose respect for him. Personal combativeness no longer stirs love and admiration in orderly and cultured circles.

If we have wrought such a change in our appraisal of persons, we can do likewise in our attitude toward nations. We can come to give our cheers to the patriots of peace as well as to those of war. We can educate ourselves to feel the thrill of pride and love when our country is showing her helpfulness with her gifts and service rather than when she is showing her hurtfulness with her guns and ships. If our schools and homes and churches set themselves to it, they can give patriotism as colorful a content in peace as in war.

If we are to fight for fellowship as men have waged war, there is a second factor which we shall have to take over into peace times. That is propaganda. Propaganda, like patriotism, has hitherto been the ally of the war-makers. It has been far more effective in the fomenting of fear and hatred than in the generating of good will. One great newspaper some time ago admitted that propaganda required hostile emotions to spur it. We can fill our largest auditoriums when we organize "anti" meetings of protest against some nation, some race, some "ism." But meetings for the promotion of charities or missions require the most artificial stimulation to draw even a modest audience.

It would seem that our fears and angers are more easily kindled than our loves. The question is, can we take propaganda over into the peace movement? Can we use it as a uniting, as well as a dividing, instrument? Or can we beget the spirit of unity within groups without playing on the fear of other groups? The ancient tribe stressed the fear of other tribes in order to hold the loyalty of its members. Political parties within nations have depended on the motives of rivalry and fear to hold their members. And this principle has even pervaded the precincts of religious groups. Sectarian groups have stirred the most fanatical loyalty by playing up the fears of rival sects.

If we can find no way of developing loyalty except through fear and hatred of others, then the vicious circles of strife within nations and between nations will go on. Recently I asked a distinguished Roman Catholic layman if he could see any hope of changing this traditional technique. He suggested that I make a study of Francis of Assisi. It is eminently worth remembering that Francis lived in the time of the Crusades. And in the contrast between the saint and the leaders of the Crusades may be seen an epitome of the choice which confronts our post-war generation. The Crusaders aroused Europe to a frenzy of hatred against the Moslems who held the Holy City, and in the effort to rescue the Holy Sepulchre from the hated infidel they decimated the homes of Europe even of their children and they drenched the hills of Palestine with the blood of both Christians and Moslems. Francis, on the other hand, contemplated the love of Christ until he caught the glow of his spirit, which he went about radiating. The quiet saint of Assisi did not have the spectacular arousing power of Peter the Hermit, but his radiance lasted longer.

Yes, propaganda for brotherhood can be effective if we set ourselves to it assiduously. Charitableness, like charity, must begin at home. Good will requires grace of action to be

effective. Friendly racial, religious, and national attitudes are
hindered by awkwardness of application as much as by lack of
good intention. Men may be committed to the theory of tolerance and yet most inept in showing the spirit of fellowship.
They are often patronizing in their tolerance, and their good
will is a synthetic product, not a delicate flowering of the human spirit. For that delicate natural flowering of good will
the home is the best, the almost indispensable soil. The experiences of the playground, the contacts of school, the news
of the world broadcast into our living rooms—these all become material for distilling good will in the alembic of the
well-run home.

The school, the church, and all community agencies must
also play their part in the propaganda for peace. It is in these
local laboratories that we test the formulas for the large solutions. Our means of communication have reduced the world
to a stage which we literate folk demand to see entire each
day. But in order to compass the global stage daily, the press
and radio must generalize. When the White House speaks,
Europe says that is America talking. When Downing Street
speaks, we say that is England talking. When the Kremlin issues a news release, the non-Soviet world says that is Russia
speaking. But the Soviet Union is more than the Kremlin, England is more than Downing Street, America is more than the
White House. And the peacemakers must see behind the broad-
casts and headlines to the human values.

The Archbishop of Canterbury in a war-time broadcast
declared that, "this world can be saved from political chaos
and collapse by one thing only, and that is worship." At first
such a statement suggests an ecclesiastic, pleading for church
attendance. But ponder the Archbishop's definition of worship, get the range and depth of it, and you will see its bearing

on the problem of peacemaking. It reads: "To worship is to quicken the conscience by the holiness of God, to feed the mind with the truth of God, to purge the imagination by the beauty of God, to open the heart to the love of God, to devote the will to the purpose of God."

To get the force of those phrases, let us run them slowly over in our minds again.

To worship is "to quicken the conscience by the holiness of God." Here are our consciences like watches run down and out of condition. We bring them to God, the One altogether holy, to be wound up, cleaned, and reconditioned.

To worship is "to feed the mind with the truth of God." We bring our minds filled with false reports, with prejudice and propaganda, yet starved for the vitamins of truth, and hungry for good news; and God feeds us with the facts that good is stronger than evil, that truth outlasts the lie, that courage is better than fear, that faith is truer than doubt.

To worship is "to purge the imagination by the beauty of God." We bring our imaginations stained with impurity, littered with the cheap and the vulgar, darkened with distrust; and God cleanses the thoughts of our hearts, replaces the pictures of battles with scenes of beauty, reveals the loveliness of virtue, lets in the light of heaven.

To worship is "to open the heart to the love of God." We bring our hearts closed against the winter of war, sometimes barred with bitterness; and in the presence of God they open to the glimpses of his love as revealed in the good earth, the fidelities of family loyalties, the beauty of Bethlehem, the last full measure of devotion on the cross.

To worship is "to devote the will to the purpose of God." We bring our wills, wayward, stubborn, rebellious, selfish;

and in the presence of God we dedicate them to his service, we align them with his loving purpose.

When we think of worship as meaning all these things, we begin to agree with the Archbishop that it is an essential part of the preface to peace. Such worship prepares the mind of the peacemaker.

The word "enlistment," like patriotism and propaganda, has a military connotation. It conjures up the sight of uniforms and the sound of marching men. In war we make individual participation so concrete that it comes home to the least and last citizen. Everyone is made to feel that he can do something—buy a bond, save sugar, conserve gasoline, take on an extra responsibility. But to speak of enlisting in the cause of peace sounds like an airy generalization. Peacemaking is so nebulous that the individual asks with a shrug of his shoulders, "What can I do about it?" Hence in war we put our shoulders to the wheel; and then when peace comes we only shrug our shoulders.

To hear without doing is worse than futile. It is disintegrating. To go on getting glimpses of challenging goals and feeling the urge of good impulses without translating them into action undermines character. That is why Matthew's gospel ends the account of the Sermon on the Mount with the warning: "Everyone that heareth these sayings of mine and doeth them not shall be likened unto a foolish man which built his house upon the sand." The foundations of character disintegrate when we go on hearing without doing. This is a point of danger for our day. Through the radio, the press, the motion pictures, and the stage we hear and see the needs and challenges of the whole world. We are made spectators of so much suffering that we grow callous to it. Ours can easily become the shallowing emotionalism of the habitual theater-goer.

During war every day's news brings glimpses of greatness, flashes of heroism, examples of human endurance which we hardly thought possible. These revelations of bravery and sacrifice are like the lightning flashes in a storm. They reveal the greatness resident in men. And the challenge of the peace-maker is to live up to the potentialities which brave men show in war. As Ben Franklin discovered electricity in a thunder-storm, so the followers of Christ can take these lightning flashes of heroism and harness them into the power needed for peace-making.

Beyond Peace of Mind

There is a peace of mind which we can understand the world may give to a man. A family is gathered for the evening meal in a comfortable home. The hush of eventide has quieted the day's activities. Bodies which have been healthily exercised are now restfully relaxed. No danger lurks to disturb the thoughts. No financial worries threaten the morrow. In such a delicious sense of physical well-being and mental content-ment, we can understand the father or mother looking around the family circle and saying, "Now this is what I call peace."

But when Jesus says, "My peace I give unto you," he is speaking out of a totally different setting. He is met in an upper room with the comrades who have weathered with him the attacks of adversity and ridicule. The air of the city is electric with the gathering storm which is to break around him in all its fury on the morrow. He knows the pain which is being prepared for him. His sensitive imagination can feel in advance the excruciating torture of the cross. Treason has entered the ranks of his most trusted friends, and one is already on the way to plot his arrest. Out of such a situation come the words, "My peace I give unto you." Surely it was hardly necessary for him to add, "Not as the world giveth, give I unto you." For whatever peace Jesus felt at that moment was beyond the power of the world to give or take away.

Such peace can come only to a person who is at one with God, his will so surrendered to God that there is no conflict of purpose, his heart so attuned that there is no disharmony of desire. When we are so at one and at work with God, we feel so at home with him that disaster, even death, cannot destroy our peace, because we have something we can take with us to God who "is our dwelling place in all generations even from everlasting to everlasting."

VIII. Having the Right Enemies

*Blessed are they which are persecuted for right-
eousness' sake: for theirs is the kingdom of heaven.*

TO BE "picked on" is a heartbreaking experience for a
child on the playground. A vivid instance comes to mind.
A certain boy because of his irascible temper and rather slow
wit became the butt of his schoolmates' jokes and the victim
of their pranks. To make matters worse his irate father would
frequently descend on the school to take his son's part. The
poor lad's life was made miserable and his attitude toward
others was left misshapen. Some youth have been led even to
self-destruction by such treatment.

The pain of being persecuted remains acute when one becomes an adult. We are made to love and be loved. We like
to be liked. Fellowship is the native air of our spirits. Our
pugnacious impulses may seem to enjoy occasional excursions
into the realms of active hostility. It is sometimes said of a
man that he "loves nothing better than a good fight." But
persecution is something different from a "good fight." To be
persecuted is to live in an atmosphere of suffocating suspicion,
to have one's private castles of security invaded by intrigue, to
be pursued by persons in a malignant spirit, to be sniped
at by enemies lying in wait, to be hounded and harassed with
unjust penalities for alleged offenses. Among all the ills that
flesh and spirit are heir to, persecution can come about the
nearest to making life a hell on earth.

Hence the last of our Lord's Beatitudes seems perhaps the

most paradoxical of all. "Blessed are they which are persecuted for righteousness' sake: for theirs is the kingdom of heaven." Then Jesus goes on to make specific and personal application of his statement, saying: "Blessed are ye, when men shall revile you and persecute you and say all manner of evil against you falsely for my sake. Rejoice and be exceeding glad, for great is your reward in heaven; for so persecuted they the prophets which were before you."

This Beatitude is hard to believe not only because to us persecution seems the very opposite of happiness, but also because it sounds strange on the lips of the compassionate Jesus, whose heart went out in incomparable sympathy to those who suffered. He it was who came "to heal the broken-hearted," and "to set at liberty them that are bruised." He looked out upon his poor countrymen carrying burdens bitterly heavy, even without special persecution, and cried: "Come unto me, all ye that labor and are heavy laden, and I will give you rest." Hence it is hard to think of his healing hands leading his already burdened followers into situations where the lash of persecution would be added. Certainly the crosses which his disciples had to bear before and after his death must have been a continuing Calvary to him. How then are we to understand Jesus when he congratulates those who are persecuted and bids them rejoice in such suffering?

WHY THE PERSECUTION?

The first consideration is to ask why they are persecuted. The mere fact of being persecuted is no proof of virtue and is worthy of no blessing in itself. When we find others against us, we should not jump to the conclusion that we are suffering for righteousness' sake. More people suffer for the wrong than for the right. When the raw recruit is out of step with the rest of his marching squad, his first need is to listen to the music and see if he be not at fault. Perhaps we may say that the first value of persecution is to induce self-examination in order to find out why others dislike us.

This need suggests a possible reason for Matthew's listing this as the last of the Beatitudes. Before we conclude that we are being persecuted for our righteousness, we should study ourselves in the light of the preceding Beatitudes. Are we sufficiently selfless to be called "poor in spirit," seeking to enrich life without greedily grabbing things for ourselves? Are we among those who mourn penitently for our own sins and sympathetically for the sufferings of others? Are we so God-trained and God-tempered that we can be called meek, because we are humble enough to be teachable and tolerant? Are we merciful to those in our power? Do we really hunger and thirst after goodness? Are we pure in heart, with will and eye and mind, single to the good, the true, the beautiful? Are we peacemakers, radiating the spirit of reconciliation, or discord makers, spreading the spirit of divisiveness? When we put these questions to ourselves, do we not have to admit that it is our faults rather than our virtues which are responsible for most of the criticism and opposition we meet? Yes, far more frequently we suffer because we are wrong than because we are right.

Nevertheless, some are persecuted for righteousness' sake. Jesus embodied the Beatitudes to perfection. Yet he was hated and hounded even to his death. Unlike the Pharisees, he did not parade his virtues before men in a provocative way of showing how much better he was than others. He was "meek and lowly in heart." His was not a hard unfeeling righteousness concerned primarily with keeping rules, but rather it was a warm, appealing goodness with an eye to the welfare of persons. He never sacrificed personalities on the altar of principles. Yet in spite of the winsomeness of his way and what Matthew Arnold called "the sweet reasonableness of Jesus," he was persecuted with unspeakable cruelty.

Jesus counselled his disciples against arousing needless antagonism. He said to them: "I send you forth as sheep in the midst of wolves; be ye therefore wise as serpents and harmless as doves," which was his figurative way of stressing the need of tact and understanding. He bade his followers not to force themselves on those who did not want them. Yet with all tact and self-restraint, Christlike goodness did and does arouse cruel opposition.

Superior goodness stirs disbelief and dislike because it disturbs the inertia of those who are set in their ways of thought and life. Pioneers in every realm are met with skepticism. Halford Luccock reminds us that when Orville and Wilbur Wright made the first airplane flight at Kitty Hawk, North Carolina, one of their neighbors in Dayton, Ohio, on hearing the news is reported to have said: "I don't believe it. Nobody's ever going to fly; and if anybody did fly, it wouldn't be anybody from Dayton." The logic of the last remark is typical of the mental littleness which lies in wait for pioneers and prophets, especially in their own country.

And in the moral and spiritual realm, those who forge ahead of the established pattern arouse a fiercer antagonism because they can be charged with disturbing sacred things. When Jesus turned to certain of the old commandments and declared: "Ye have heard it was said by them of old time . . . but I say unto you," he was heading for trouble. His critics found it easy to convince the conservatives that Jesus was a blasphemer and an iconoclast. To them he was undermining their foundations. Others besides Nicodemus may have been wise enough to discern the rightness and divine origin of Jesus' teachings; but they were too cowed by the crowd's opinion to let their views be known. It was dangerous to be thought a "fellow-traveler" when Jesus was the enemy within the gates.

The haunting sense of rightness which superior goodness arouses often only serves to heighten the opposition of the conventionally and conservatively good. When a person goes ahead of them in goodness, some are sure to talk about "being too good to be true." They try to tone down the demands of his high ethics. They bid him use "common sense," which means conforming to crowd morality. Instead of pulling themselves up to the higher level, they try to pull the better characters down by ridicule and persecution. As in Tolstoi's experience, the moral pioneer or spiritual prophet stands alone in his search after virtue. When he tries to express the longings of his heart for a truly virtuous life, he is met with contempt and derisive laughter.

When a person is not too good, he is called "a good fellow," and the crowd laughs with him. When he sets his moral standards high above his neighbors', they laugh at him and call him a fool or a fanatic. Thus the crowd stones prophets and tries to pull the saints from their pedestals. When the Jerusalem mob called for the release of Barabbas rather than Jesus, Matthew records that even Pilate recognized that they did what they did through envy. Jesus manifested a goodness which the people secretly envied but refused to emulate. They freed Barabbas, who eased their consciences by arousing their passions against a foreign foe. They killed "the pioneer of life," who disturbed their peace of mind with his divine goodness.

Moreover, Christlike goodness is persecuted not only because it is a standing rebuke to the conventionally good, but also because it interferes with those who want to be bad. Superficial thinkers may assume that the virtues described in the Beatitudes—mercy, meekness, purity of heart, and the like —are so weak and gentle that they are harmless and arouse no opposition. Quite the opposite. The pure in heart who insist on truth and goodness interfere with those who follow their prejudices and passions. The merciful, when they advocate forgiveness while the crowd is crying for vengeance, are denounced as weaklings, soft sentimentalists. The peacemakers who pursue a course of reconciliation past the point where hotheads call for war, are reviled as traitors and scorned by their fellow citizens.

The righteous are a standing rebuke to wrongdoers. They haunt them with their higher goodness as the beatific smile of the stoned Stephen haunted Saul of Tarsus. They exercise a silent veto, and though the unrighteous may override it, the effect is not erased. The man who refuses to sell his soul for an unworthy cause arouses the resentment of its promoters as Naboth's refusal to part with his vineyard incurred the ire of Ahab and Jezebel.

John Galsworthy in his drama "The Mob" depicted a rising young politician who disapproved of his government's policy toward a smaller nation. He spoke out on the subject. His political colleagues counselled him to keep silent or he would jeopardize his future. His wife warned him that if he persisted in his outspoken opposition, she would leave him. But he would not be muzzled. He ruined his political career. His wife did desert him. He was killed by a mob. But he refused to sell his soul for silence.

Public men who stand for great principles have to run the gauntlet of persecution somewhere along the line. Gladstone championed Home Rule for Ireland. That stand cost him the leadership of his party and alienated many of his friends. What he stood for was later conceded, but Gladstone was in his grave for two decades before the seed which he planted began to appear above ground. It took half a century for the clouds of calumny to clear away so that men could see Abraham Lincoln objectively. And Dean Sperry says that it will be another generation before Woodrow Wilson can be studied in clear perspective.

When Jesus was reviled, he reviled not again; but his silence did not mean his surrender to the principles of those who persecuted him. He kept on taking out the sin rather than "taking it out" on the sinner. He said, "I came not to send peace but a sword." Christ would have his followers fight for righteousness with spiritual rather than physical weapons but with a heroism, ingenuity, and devotion matching that of the warrior in battle. The Christian is called to be "a good soldier of Jesus Christ." This means that he must "stand, and having done all to stand." It means also that he must advance, pushing the principles of Christlike goodness up to the advancing frontiers of human experience. It means taking the Ten Commandments and lengthening their points to prick the conscience with the awareness of new social sins. It means illuminating the Golden Rule with imagination so that those who presume to practice it will know what they would want done to them if they were in the other person's place.

When a man sets out to live Christ's kind of goodness, he can still expect to be persecuted for righteousness' sake. Methods may have been refined, but the pain is no less real; the blood of Christian martyrs has been shed even in the twentieth century. Studdert-Kennedy, gallant British Chaplain of World War I, gave our generation too much credit for tolerance, when he wrote that "when Jesus came to Golgotha, they hanged him on a tree" but "when Jesus came to Birmingham, they simply passed him by." Of course, as Kennedy pointed out, Jesus preferred physical torture to indifference, because to be ignored is the worst form of persecution to one who really cares for his cause.

But the generation that produced a Hitler can hardly claim to treat Christ with polite indifference. The trial of Christ is being prosecuted today with far more diabolical skill than in Pilate's court. Ideologies, like those of communism and fascism, are arrayed against the principles of Jesus. Billions are being spent to defeat the things Jesus stood for. And those who espouse his cause in concrete issues still meet with ridicule, reviling and persecution because they disturb the conventionally good and interfere with the determinedly bad.

REVEALING THE REAL STUFF

And now what are the blessings of the persecuted? For one thing, the opposition we meet in pursuit of righteousness reveals that we have the real stuff of goodness in us. A radio letter recently asked how can a person know when he is saved. The question savors a bit too much of self-interest. Jesus made clear the basic test of discipleship: "By this shall all men know that ye are my disciples, if ye have love one to another."

But if you want to know whether you belong to the company of God's elect, you can test your membership both by how much you love and by how much you are opposed, even hated. Have you ever been good enough to be persecuted for your goodness? If you never stand up for anything which somebody wants to knock down, if you never say anything which somebody does not criticize, if your righteousness has never aroused any ridicule or reviling, if all men speak well of you—then beware, because you do not bear the mark of God's true servants in the past.

A man is known by the enemies he makes as truly as by the friends he keeps. Dwight L. Moody was wont to say that when any considerable time passed without someone attacking him, he became concerned about the vitality of his message. A live religious message gives light to the faithful; it also strikes sparks when something interferes with its current.

Bishop Eivind Bergrav of Oslo was interned by the Nazis during their occupation of Norway. Speaking later of his experience, he said:

In prison we had our Bibles but we were literally at war with the Gestapo on account of them. When I myself was interned and was allowed to send a short letter to my wife each week, I wrote after the First Sunday in Advent, 1942: The Gospel for yesterday was remarkable: "I am come to set the captives at liberty, to bring freedom to the oppressed." My wife was then called before the chief of police and told that her husband was henceforth forbidden to quote the Bible. "The Bible is much too topical."

God's word is topical for all men, even for those who are said to be unbelievers—though more men believe than are themselves aware of the fact so that even these so-called unbelievers found the Bible to be something extraordinary. If a man merely caught sight of a Bible lying on a table, he felt: "There is the toughest reality in the world."

Most certainly in time of persecution God's word becomes a living power in the soul of a people.

Norway's experience is not without parallel in practically every land which has suffered persecution for its faith. Fire tests the quality of our faith, whether it be "gold, silver, precious stones, wood, hay, stubble." The springs of spiritual refreshment are rediscovered and reopened. Those who in their comfortable days complained of the church as a burden to support rediscover under persecution that vital religion is a boon to support them.

George Eliot in *Middlemarch* speaks of the exhilaration felt by those who know themselves guiltless before a condemning crowd. It is the exaltation of spirit which caused Paul and Silas to sing as they lay chained in prison. It is the high confidence which sustained Hugh Latimer as he went to the stake, calling to his fellow martyr: "Be of good cheer, Master Ridley, and play the man: we shall this day light such a candle by God's grace in England as shall never be put out."

When a follower of Christ tries to rise toward his Lord's high goodness, he finds in opposition what the flier finds in a headwind, namely that which enables him to get off the ground. A headwind slows the speed of the plane in the air, but it is essential for rising and landing. When the prophet of God wishes to bring his message down to earth on some concrete issue, he can usually locate the most vital spots by the opposition he meets. A tramp explained his course of travel by saying that he always kept the wind at his back. That fact also serves to explain why the tramp never lands a lasting job or joy.

SOULS NOT FOR SALE

Furthermore, those who endure persecution for righteousness' sake not only discover whether they have the real stuff of goodness in them, but they thereby develop it. When a man stands up to duty in the face of opposition, he cultivates a compactness of character. A tough core of reality begins to form in his inner self. It is just the opposite of that flabbiness which was the fate of Peer Gynt, who always went around his obstacles rather than through them. Ibsen portrays the result in showing Peer's character as resembling an onion, layer after layer peeling off leaving a central core of nothingness.

A spiritual leader of our time, Justin Wroe Nixon, recounts how he found the reality of his trust in God. He risked his future by taking his stand on a difficult moral issue. He said that at first it was like stepping into quicksand. He seemed to go down and down until the dire consequences threatened to engulf him. Then it was as if his foot struck solid ground, and he found that underneath were the everlasting arms.

When we resist the temptation to sell our souls under pressure of persecution, we get a new sense of possessing our souls. We feel a new mastery of ourselves. Suppose that a teacher is subjected to certain pressure groups which insist that he color his teaching according to their desires. In order to please these groups, he prostitutes the truth. He may thereby hold his position, but he has put a mortgage on his soul. He can no longer quite call his soul his own. But suppose he resists the temptation. He thereby gains entrance to the kingdom of truth, which Jesus was revealing when Pilate asked him, "Art thou a king?" Jesus replied: "To this end was I born and for this cause came I into the world, that I should bear witness unto the truth. Everyone that is of the truth heareth my voice." The teacher who stands by the truth, cost what it may, hears the King's voice, for he is in the Kingdom where truth reigns.

The selling of one's soul under pressure may be so subtly done that others may not know it. But down in the depths of his heart the seller knows that there is a yellow streak. And the thought of the yellowness spreads decay in his soul as the presence of one rotten apple in a barrel radiates rottenness, or as the memory of his cowardice in deserting his ship gnawed at the soul of Conrad's Lord Jim. A man may yield to the fear of persecution by merely keeping silence, as guests often do at dinner tables when false rumors are going around or reputations are being gossiped away, or as popular preachers sometimes do by steering clear of sensitive subjects and speaking loudly on safe themes. No one else may suspect that they have run away from a moral fight, but they in their more searching moments are aware of the weakness within.

Suppose, however, they stand up to the dangerous issue, not evading it even by silence. Then there comes a sense of integrity like that felt by Job, when he climaxed the evidence of his honesty by asking God to judge, "If ever I kept quiet within doors, afraid of what the crowd would say, dreading public opinion." The man who can say that feels that he can call his soul his own.

When a person can say as Paul said in his defense before King Agrippa, "I was not disobedient unto the heavenly vision"; when he has not tried to tone down the moral ruggedness of Christ's commands into a comfortable common sense; when he has not quit the struggle despite the fierceness of his foes and the fickleness of his friends; when he has risen from his bed of stones and gone back to the Lystrans which stoned him—then like Paul he develops an indissoluble union with divine love and can say: "Who shall separate us from the love of Christ? shall tribulation, or distress, or persecution, or famine, or nakedness, or peril, or sword? . . . Nay, in all these things we are more than conquerors through him that loved us."

WHERE GOODNESS BECOMES CREATIVE

Not only an inner exaltation of spirit and a new soundness of character, but a still further blessing comes to those who endure persecution for righteousness' sake. Their goodness becomes creative. Situations which seemed closed begin to break open with promise.

A young minister in a New England industrial town was on the point of leaving his parish. He was a man of refined taste and sensitive temperament. He loved the aesthetic and sought to cultivate in his congregation a spirit of worship. He enriched the church services with liturgy. But all this seemed lost on his congregation. A call came to a larger city where his type of ministry would be more appreciated. But he stuck by his parish. And then things began to break for him. Hearts that were cold seemed to grow warm toward him. He discovered in unexpected places an appreciation of what he was trying to do.

A wife was about to leave her husband. He had made life pretty much of a hell for her. Her acquaintances put him down as a "washout." But she still believed there was a vein of gold in him. She kept on prospecting in the mine which others bade her abandon. And then she struck something rich enough to pay off. The home held together until death parted them, and the latter years had the serenity of a beautiful sunset.

Love longs to sacrifice for its beloved. A mother's heart expands when she can "put herself out" for her child. We prize our love according to what it costs us. Hence there is an ascetic principle at the heart of all the great ethnic religions. A religion could not be great without that element of sacrifice, for it otherwise would not reach the deepest need of human nature, which is the need to be needed. And Christianity demonstrates its superiority over other faiths because its central symbol is the Cross.

But taking up the cross is more than bearing manfully the

burdens which are the common lot of mortal men. To carry one's cross means assuming responsibilities which could have been evaded. It requires fortitude to endure the painful load plus love to forgive those who thus tax us. Christ's cross-carriers are called to love their enemies, to bless those that curse them, to do good to those that hate them, to pray for those who despitefully use them and persecute them. Such demands seem at first to be moral impossibles. And practical men say, surely God meant us to use common sense. But as Arthur Clutton-Brock says: "Something greater, more beautiful, more passionate, than common sense is needed, if we are to have common sense. . . . This is the paradox of the Christian virtues. Common sense will not lead you to practise them; you must see their beauty as something divine and worthy of sacrifice, and then they will lead you to common sense."

The unlisted Beatitude, "It is more blessed to give than to receive," is unbelievable to the amateur giver. But if one keeps on practicing the art of giving, there comes a point when the joy of it is revealed. Music lessons are a distasteful discipline to the little girl during her first weeks at the keyboard, but there comes a time when music "gets" her, and what was a load becomes a lift.

Likewise in the face of persecution, when you stand, and having done all, still stand; when you turn the other cheek and go the second mile; when you persist in praying for those who despitefully use you; then says Jesus, you show yourselves "children of your Father which is in heaven." And when you thus realize your sonship, Paul out of his painful experience declares that you feel yourselves "heirs of God and joint-heirs with Jesus Christ." Then we are getting within the kingdom of love, wherein is found the higher happiness.

When we hold on to our faith and persist in our serving and forgiving spirit until we are "at the end of our string," as we say, and then still hold on, we touch One "able to do exceeding abundantly above all that we ask or think, according to the power that worketh in us."

THE GOODLY COMPANY OF THE GALLANT

Among the other blessings which come to those who are persecuted for righteousness' sake is that they enter into the fellowship of gallant souls, and thereby reinforce their own faith. Jesus seemed to have this in mind when he added to this eighth Beatitude the words: "Rejoice and be exceeding glad; . . . for so persecuted they the prophets which were before you." When going is difficult, it does help to feel that we are traveling where the saints have trod. Hence we are confident that the road must lead on, even though it be hidden from our eyes by fears and fog.

When Lady Astor made her maiden speech in Parliament, it required considerable courage both because she was breaking an ancient tradition as the first woman member of Parliament and because she stood for an unpopular attitude toward the liquor traffic. Yet note how the new member from Plymouth revealed her own sources of encouragement and sought to convince her colleagues:

Honorable members, however, should not be frightened of what Plymouth sends out into the world. After all, I suppose when Drake and Raleigh wanted to set out on their venturesome careers, some cautious persons said, "Stay at home cruising in home waters." I have no doubt that the same thing occurred when the Pilgrim Fathers set out. I have no doubt that there were cautious brethren who did not understand their going out into the wide seas to worship God in their own way. But on the whole, the world is all the better for those venturesome and courageous West Country people.

Yes, the pioneer spirits, both secular and spiritual, have been lonely pilgrims of a hard path, but they have prepared the way of the Lord and made straight in the desert the high-way of our God. Suppose no Francis of Assisi had risked ridi-cule to leaven with love the sodden mass of medieval cruelty. Suppose no John Howard had opposed the conservatives of his time to cleanse the prison conditions. Suppose no Wil-liam Wilberforce had been willing to suffer scorn in the effort to rid England of the African slave traffic. Heroic souls like these may well come to mind when we are tempted to say: "Why bother about trying to better this bad world? All that can be expected of us is to be decent and let the devil take the hindmost."

Had it not been for those who went beyond the paved roads of conventional goodness and cut across hostile coun-try to reach the higher righteousness, there would be no society where even the commonly good could find a decent and satis-fying place to live. Our Christian order, imperfect as it is, has been advanced by those who demonstrated a goodness more dynamic than mere decency and a righteousness that risked the reviling of the merely respectable.

And those who have been persecuted for righteousness' sake constitute a glad and gallant company, who "having ob-tained a good report through faith, received not the promise: God having provided some better thing for us that they with-out us should not be made perfect." Life is like a relay race. Others have run before us, and we start from the point where their lives touch ours. We are linked with them for their sakes and for ours.

At the 1948 Olympic games in London occurred a dramatic incident, among several. In a relay race, the French team had started well. But as the baton was being passed to one of the subsequent runners, he dropped it. The accident, of course, put the team out of the running. The runner at fault dropped to the ground, flung his hands to his head in a gesture of despair and openly wept. His emotional outburst continued as he was led from the arena. To take defeat so tearfully might seem a bit unsportsmanlike, were it not remembered how many persons were involved in that runner's failure. There were his watching compatriots with their dashed hopes. There were the two teammates who had run before him and whose work was ruined by his blunder. And then there was the runner who was to come after, but who never got the chance to run at all.

Our lives on this earth do not begin with our birth or end with our death. As Edmund Burke said, society is a compact between the living, the dead, and the great unborn. To keep faith with those who have gone before and those who are to come after is the mark of a gentleman. A Christian must be a gentleman, and more. "The honor of the service" calls for endurance through weariness and courage under persecution.

But let those who overcome "rejoice and be exceeding glad; for so persecuted they the prophets which were before you." Seeing that we are compassed about with such a gallant company, "let us run with patience the race that is set before us, looking unto Jesus the author and finisher of our faith, who for the joy that was set before him endured the cross, despising the shame, and is set down at the right hand of the throne of God."

References

Page	Line	Reference
11	21	Luke 4:18-19.
12	9	Arnold Toynbee, *A Study of History*, abridged by D. C. Somervell (New York: Oxford Univ. Press, 1947), p. 439.
12	11	Luke 17:21.
12	19	*Sartor Resartus*, Book II, Chap. IX.
13	1	Luke 16:13; Mark 3:25.
13	6	Matt. 6:33.
15	5	Matt. 11:25.
15	30	New York: Charles Scribner's Sons, 1948. P. 116.
19	1	Epistle Dedicatory to *Man and Superman*.
20	14	John 16:33.
20	28	Ps. 31:20.
21	17	I Cor. 9:27.
22	15	Matt. 6:20.
25	7	*Christian Behavior* (New York: The Macmillan Co., 1943), pp. 45, 48.
27	19	*Life and Letters*, I, 219.
30	31	II Chron. 26:15, 16.
33	9	Rom. 1:14.
33	20	*Power: A New Social Analysis* (New York: W. W. Norton & Co., 1938), p. 11.
34	6	Matt. 5:16, italics mine.
37	8	*Freedom's People* (New York: Harper & Bros., 1945), pp. 39-40.
40	8	II Cor. 7:10.
43	5	Elbert Russell, *The Beatitudes* (New York: Harper & Bros., 1929), p. 43.
45	30	G. Lowes Dickinson, *A Modern Symposium* (New York: Doubleday, Page & Co., 1905), p. 99.

Page	Line	Reference
46	24	Lincoln Barnett, "God and the American People" (*Ladies' Home Journal*, November, 1948).
48	4	John 15:11.
48	7	John 15:3.
48	22	Num. 14:18.
49	32	*The Return to Religion* (New York: The Macmillan Co., 1936), p. 23.
52	31	John 16:33.
54	22	Published by Rinehart & Co.
55	14	II Cor. 1:3-4.
55	20	I Cor. 15:26.
55	24	John 20:29.
56	29	John 14:2.
59	26	"Beyond the Horizon."
65	13	Matt. 11:28-30.
65	28	Ps. 37:11.
66	12	Num. 12:3.
67	3	Acts 9:4-5.
67	8	Rom. 12:11.
68	11	Zech. 4:6.
68	21	Isa. 42:3.
68	23	Isa. 40:15.
69	16	II Cor. 5:19.
70	17	John 10:17, 18.
70	25	I Cor. 1:24.
72	17	John 4:14.
73	32	I Cor. 3:22-23.
74	29	Prov. 16:32.
77	4	John 6:35.
80	19	Luke 16:8.
82	25	Matt. 22:37.
84	12	Rom. 5:7.
84	19	Matt. 5:17.
86	23	Luke 20:25.
86	28	Matt. 18:21, 22.
87	7	Heb. 13:8.
88	12	Matt. 7:7.
88	17	Luke 6:25.
88	31	Rom. 10:10.
89	15	John 14:14.

Page	Line	Reference
89	21	Gal. 5:22-23.
92	7	New York: The Vanguard Press, 1939. P. 80.
92	29	Luke 11:5-8.
94	6	Rev. 3:8.
94	18	*A Man Can Live* (New York: Harper & Bros., 1947), p. 22.
95	6	Matt. 6:31-33.
107	7	Matt. 5:44-45.
107	27	John 3:16.
108	17	Luke 7:47.
109	7	Matt. 7:1.
109	20	*On Final Ground* (New York: Harper & Bros., 1946), p. 158.
110	16	Heb. 4:16.
110	19	Rev. 4:3.
112	2	Prov. 25:21, 22; Rom. 12:20.
113	9	John 8:3-11.
115	10	Luke 6:37-38.
115	13	James Russell Lowell, *Sonnet IV*.
116	8	Eph. 3:20.
117	15	Mark 8:18.
120	16	Matt. 16:6.
120	31	Rom. 12:2.
122	8	II Cor. 1:19.
122	11	John 5:17.
122	12	John 14:12.
122	14	John 16:13.
122	18	John 14:2.
122	24	P. 547.
123	27	Eph. 1:17.
124	27	I Cor. 2:14.
125	15	Jas. 4:8.
126	4	*Purity XIX*, p. 26.
126	8	John 7:17.
127	11	Matt. 6:22.
127	18	John 18:37.
128	7	Ps. 19:1.
129	17	Gen. 32:30.
130	4	Job 42:5.
130	12	I Cor. 2:2.

Page	Line	Reference
130	14	Phil. 1:21.
130	17	II Tim. 1:12.
133	30	Mark 3:25.
135	11	Luke 9:62.
135	19	Luke 9:60.
136	8	Rom. 7:19, 22-23.
137	9	Jas. 3:17.
137	19	Jas. 3:18.
137	28	I Cor. 13:11, 13.
138	12	II Cor. 5:19.
138	13	II Cor. 5:18.
138	30	Eph. 4:15.
140	19	Matt. 18:3.
141	28	Matt. 5:44-45.
142	8	Published by the Macmillan Co., and used by their permission.
144	7	I John 1:7.
144	21	Matt. 10:34.
150	24	Matt. 7:26.
154	13	Luke 4:18.
154	17	Matt. 11:28.
155	29	Matt. 11:29.
156	6	Matt. 10:16.
156	28	Matt. 5:27-28.
156	32	John 3:2.
157	24	Matt. 27:18.
157	28	Acts 3:15, Moffatt translation.
159	12	Matt. 10:34.
160	21	John 13:35.
161	30	I Cor. 3:12-13.
163	22	John 18:37.
164	13	Job 31:34, Moffatt translation.
164	25	Rom. 8:35-37.
166	17	Acts 20:35.
166	28	Matt. 5:45.
166	30	Rom. 8:17.
167	3	Eph. 3:20.
167	11	Matt. 5:12.
169	27	Heb. 12:1-2.